THE CLARKS OF KENTUCKY

Cover Photo by Doulas C. Harrison—The Falls of the Ohio River as they exist today (below the dam).

THE CLARKS OF KENTUCKY

DOUGLAS C. HARRISON

iUniverse, Inc.
Bloomington

THE CLARKS OF KENTUCKY

iUniverse books may be ordered through booksellers or by contacting:

iUniverse
1663 Liberty Drive
Bloomington, IN 47403
www.iuniverse.com
1-800-Authors (1-800-288-4677)

ISBN: 978-1-4620-5858-7 (sc)
ISBN: 978-1-4620-5859-4 (ebk)

Printed in the United States of America

iUniverse rev. date: 11/11/2011

CONTENTS

ACKNOWLEDGMENTS

To my beautiful and brilliant daughter Dianne—a successful business executive and authoress herself—who helped me greatly with the technical part of writing a book and getting it published.

And

To my daughter Linda—a successful business woman, mother of Robyn and Laura, and grandmother of Lola (all beautiful and brilliant)—who gave me great encouragement and support while I was writing the book.

And

To my wife Joan—an excellent veteran school teacher—who helped to critique the book and correct each chapter as we went along.

FOREWORD

As most of us know, many men and women have been influential in developing America into the great nation it has become. We all know about Washington, Jefferson, Lee, Grant, both Roosevelts, Reagan, and all of the great women who supported them. In my opinion, one family has also been very influential through American history in every phase of this great trip—the Clarks of Kentucky.

From George Rogers Clark winning the Revolutionary War in the west—thus giving America the Northwest Territory, to his younger brother William Clark exploring the Louisiana Purchase with Meriwether Lewis and becoming a great Indian diplomat, from William's son Meriwether Lewis, Sr. fighting in three wars, and becoming a famous architect, and to his son Meriwether Lewis Clark, Jr. founding Churchill Downs, and starting the now world famous Kentucky Derby. I will attempt in a small way to chronicle how it all happened.

CHAPTER 1

George Rogers Clark Goes Surveying-In Western Virginia

What made people like George Rogers Clark leave the beautiful state of Virginia? It had everything according to John Smith in 1607-fertile land, adequate navigable waterways, fowl, fish, and animals to kill for food. The obvious answer is—land of their own, that which motivates most human beings. The land in Virginia in the 18th century, as in the rest of the colonies, was given by heritage, or by a kings decree to the royalty of England—since they had financed awll trips to America from the year 1800 on. Once the native Americans / Indians had been eliminated or driven westward, the small numbers of the kings favorites were given title to all of the land from the Atlantic Ocean to the west as far as it went—they had no clue how far. Virginia went as far as "Kain-tuck-e" and beyond.

For example Thomas, sixth Lord Fairfax had inherited all of the land between the headwaters of the Potomac and Rappahannock Rivers to the Chesapeake Bay. His grandfather Lord Culpepper had increased his ownership of the the area from 1,000,000 acres to 5,000,000 acres by some clever changes to the original grant. Lord Fairfax became one of the richest men in the civilized world. (Note 1)

Even before the Revolution, some large plots of land were given or sold to friends or relatives of the landed gentry. George Rogers Clark's father John Clark owned a small farm when he married Ann Rogers. Her family had apparently benefitted by the English system, by inheriting some land.

Father John Clark had become a lawyer, and had become a friend of George Mason—by defending him in a law suit. Through this friendship he also met other influential Virginians—including Thomas Jefferson.

As the second son born to John Clark and Ann Rogers, George Rogers Clark (Born November 19, 1752) grew up enjoying many benefits of a fairly well-to-do, and well connected family. He had a small amount of formal education, but was mostly home schooled—as was the norm of the day. Although farming was the main occupation of the family, George was not enamored by it. At age 19 he set out to survey parts of western Virginia—his grandfather having taught him to survey. (Note 2)

At age 20 he went farther west to survey—and to look for some land of his own—knowing that his older brother Jonathan would inherit the family plantation, due to the English law of primogeniture. Also, even a successful Virginia planter was constantly in need of more fertile land—since crop rotation had not been started—making large plots of land producing very little.

In Kentucky George had heard of thousands of acres of great fertile "cane land". At some point he met George Croghan (pronounced "Crawn"). They eventually surveyed Kentucky west to the Ohio River, and found this to be true.

As was the case of George Washington, surveying for the sixth Lord Fairfax, the surveyors were usually paid with titles to some of the land where they were surveying. Obviously they would pick out prime tracts for themselves. For example, George Washington picked out a large tract of beautiful fertile land in what is now Charles Town, West Virginia (about sixty miles west of Washington D. C.). He planned to move there, but the death of his brother Lawrence set him up with Mount Vernon. Many of his relatives did settle there in Charles Town (named for his brother Charles). Why not, since he gave them the land that he no longer needed or wanted. (Note 3)

George Rogers Clark had no such windfall, so he went west to Kentucky to eventually settle—with his partner George Croghan. George Croghan would later marry George Rogers Clark's sister Lucy, and in 1790 build their beautiful plantation home in Louisville, Kentucky—Locust Grove.

Note 1, Miriam Haynie, *The Stronghold,* (Richmond, VA, TheDietz Press, Inc., 1959), Pages 143-144.
Note 2, George Rogers Clark, Wikipedia, the free encyclopedia, Page 2.
Note 3, Charles Washington, Wikipedia, the free encyclopedia.

CHAPTER 2

Early Settlements in Kentucky

At this point in 1773, many people other than George Rogers Clark had the same idea to go west for dreams of fertile land of their own, and freedom in western Virginia—which is now Kentucky—or as the Indians called it "Kain-tuck-e" or "Ken-ta-ten". The trip was long and difficult, by way of the winding Ohio River from Pittsburg, or by land through the Cumberland Gap. Although the Indian problem was still very much prevalent, they were more active north of the Ohio River—thus the Indiana territory was named—and eventually the state name. Most Indians, however, still considered Kentucky as their happy hunting ground—and they did not want white settlers coming in to diminish the amount of game available. (Note 1)

Although George Rogers Clark eventually surveyed as far south as the Falls of the Ohio River (present day Louisville, Kentucky), his first job in Kentucky was with the Ohio Land Company, to survey the lands from the Ohio River to the settlements of Harrodsburg and Boonesboro—by way of the Kentucky River.

Virtually no settlers went down the Ohio River as far as the falls. It was a longer trip and the various Indian tribes could observe and attack white settlers more easily—from the north side of the river.

Daniel Boone was born in 1734 in western Pennsylvania. His family eventually moved to the Yadkin Valley of North Carolina (about 50 miles west of present day Greensboro, N. C.). He fought for the British in the French and Indian War. During that period he met a man named John Finley who told Boone about the fertile land and abundance of game in Kentucky. In 1769 Boone and a friend started a two-year hunting expedition into Kentucky. Later that year they were captured by Shawnees who took their bounty of skins, and told them to get out of their hunting ground—and don't come back! Not to be discouraged, Boone continued to hunt, trap, and explore in Kentucky—until his return to North Carolina in 1771.

After another hunting trip into Kentucky in 1772, Daniel Boone packed up his family and led a group of about fifty settlers through the Cumberland Gap into Kentucky—on September 25, 1873. As the settlers went north, a small group—including Boone's oldest son James—separated from the main party. On October 9, they were attacked by a band of Delawares, Shawnees, and Cherokees. The Indians had apparently decided to send a message to the white settlers—stay out of our hunting grounds. They massacred the entire group—sending shock waves back to the east. Boone and the rest of his party headed back east to the relative safety of North Carolina. This incident would cause the British government to order Lord Dunmore to organize a force to remove the Indians from Kentucky and southern Ohio. (Note 2)

Like Daniel Boone, James Harrod was born in Pennsylvania and became a frontiersman, hunter, and trapper. He also fought in the French and Indian War—probably at age 14—having been born in 1746.

While staying with the British army, Harrod was ordered by Lord Dunmore to lead an expedition into Kentucky to survey land that had been promised to British soldiers who had served in the French and Indian War. James Harrod and his 37 men left Fort Redstone near Pittsburg early in 1774. They traveled down the Monongahela and Ohio Rivers to the mouth of the Kentucky River. After going up the Kentucky and crossing the Salt River, they decided to build a fort near the two rivers. On June 16, 1774 James Harrod and his men established what would become the first permanent pioneer settlement in Kentucky. They called it Harrods Town in his honor (now Harrodsburg, about thirty miles southwest of Lexington, KY). Just as the first structures were completed, the men were ordered to go back north to fight Indians in Lord Dunmore's War. (Note 3)

Note 1, George Rogers Clark—Wikipedia, the free encyclopedia, Page 2.
Note 2, Daniel Boone—Wikipedia, the free encyclopedia, Page 4.
Note 3, James Harrod—Wikipedia, the free encyclopedia, Page 2.

CHAPTER 3

Lord Dunmore's War

In 1774 at age 22 George Rogers Clark joined the Virginia Militia at Fort Pitt, under the command of British Governor Lord Dunmore—to fight the Shawnee Indians, who had been harassing and killing settlers in Kentucky. It was there that Clark met and became friends with Simon Kenton—the great hunter and Indian scout. Lord Dunmore had 2,000 British Regular Troops, and had mustered another 1,000 Colonial troops under the command of Colonel Andrew Lewis. Unfortunately, Lord Dunmore's motive was to gain land for his personal use. He also wanted to make the Colonial troops look bad—in order to discourage American thoughts of revolution. (Note 1)

While Lord Dunmore stayed near Fort Pitt, Colonel Lewis fought a large Indian force when trapped in a triangle at Point Pleasant—it was anything but pleasant!! The Colonists fought bravely, but suffered heavy losses while pinned on a bluff between the Ohio and Kanawha Rivers (near present day Huntington and Charleston, West Virginia). Luckily the Indians became discouraged when they could not achieve a total victory, and returned to the north bank of the Ohio River. At this point the Mingo, Delaware, and the Wyandot Indians—allies of the Shawnees—decided to go home to their villages. (Note 2)

After a council meeting, the Shawnees agreed to meet with Lord Dunmore, and sign a peace treaty. Thus, the Colonial troops did the dirty work, while Lord Dunmore got the credit for attaining peace with the Indians in Kentucky. This action gave the Americans another reason to dislike the pompous British leaders. George Rogers Clark gained some military experience, but never had to fire a shot—having been attached to Lord Dunmore's part of the mission. (Note 3)

Clark would return to Kentucky and become a surveyor for the Ohio Land Company. His job was to lay out tracts of land on the Kentucky River. It was here that he would meet up with James Harrod and eventually move to Harrod's Town. Ironically James Harrod and his men had been ordered back to help with the war. Luckily for them—they arrived at the site of the Battle of Point Pleasant at midnight on October 10—the day the battle had ended. James Harrod was also lucky in that there were very few Indians in Kentucky while he was building his fort—they were very busy assembling for the battle at Point Pleasant. Unfortunately for James Harrod, Daniel Boone, and many other Kentucky settlers, the Indians would eventually break Lord Dunmore's peace treaty and cause more havoc in Kentucky. (Note 4)

Note 1, Thomas D. Clark, *Simon Kenton-Kentucky Scout,* (New York, NY, Farrar & Rinehart, 1943), Page 80.

Note 2, Lowell H. Harrison, *George Rogers Clark and the War in the west,* (Lexington, KY, The University Press of Kentucky, 1976), Pages 5-6.

Note 3, Thomas D. Clark, *A History of Kentucky,* (New York, NY, Prentice-Hall, 1937), Page 40.

Note 4, James Harrod—Wikipedia, the free encyclopedia, Page 2.

CHAPTER 4

New Leaders in Kentucky

As George Rogers Clark got settled in Harrod's Town in 1775 at age twenty-five, he rapidly became recognized as a leader by the other settlers. He was six feet tall, had flaming red hair, and talked the language of the frontiersmen as they shared their hardships. He had a flair for the dramatic, and was a skilled orator.

At this point in March of 1775, an ambitious judge—Richard Henderson from North Carolina—had a vision of taking over Kentucky and making it a separate country—with Henderson as its supreme ruler, or at least a new colony, with he as governor.

To this end, with partners, he established the Translyvania Land Company, and negotiated with the Cherokee Indians to buy most of Kentucky. He paid the Indians $10,000 in guns and provisions of all kinds. The Cherokees very cleverly did not mention that they did not own the land, but only used it under a treaty with the Shawnee. (Note 1)

A naive Daniel Boone had helped to set up the negotiations—perhaps for money or promises of glory in the new regime. As he left the treaty site, the Cherokee chief, "Dragging Canoe", shook Boone's hand but said: "We have given you a fine land brother, but you ill find it under a cloud, and a dark and bloody ground". (Note 2)

Daniel Boone left the treaty site, known as Sycamore Shoals with thirty men, and orders from Richard Henderson to establish the capitol of his Translyvania Empire. Boone found a plain near a salt lick frequented by great herds of buffalo and elk. There he and his men erected a fort, and by popular acclaim named it Boonesboro. Thus

Harrodsburg and Boonesboro became forts with rival leadership—only twenty-two miles apart as the crow flies.

On May 23, 1775, Judge Richard Henderson called a meeting at Boonesboro for all the forts to send delegates—to establish laws by which he would govern Kentucky. Needless to say, the settlers were not interested in a central all powerful dictatorial government, like England, or the present day American colonies, from whom many had endured great hardship to escape. (Note 4)

Fortunately for the settlers, George Rogers Clark was in attendance at the meeting. He wanted Kentucky to become a county of Virginia, and thus receive aid and a militia to protect it. Since the Indian problem was again getting very serious, and he was worried about his rival Judge Henderson taking over his beloved Kentucky, George Rogers Clark set out in the fall of 1775 to Williamsburg—to plead his case.

When Clark arrived in Williamsburg in December, he found that Henderson's agents were already there—lobbying Congress to approve his illegal contract with the Indians. Fortunately George Rogers Clark's persuasive oratory convinced Congress to consider creating the county of Kentucky—from the westward portion of the Fincastle County lands.

At this point the Continental Congress of Virginia was busy with matters of the impending revolution. They became irritated By Judge Henderson's claims of land ownership from the Cherokees—that still belonged to Virginia. What better way to squelch a "landpyrate" (as Henderson had been accused of being in North Carolina) than to give power to a native Virginian—with a well known and respected Virginia family. Thus, George Rogers Clark was given the task of returning to Williamsburg with the elected delegates from the western part of Fincastle County.

Clark quickly agreed to their terms, and sent scout messingers to Kentucky to meet at Harrod's Town on June 6, 1776 to pursue the matter. Although George Rogers Clark returned to Kentucky in the spring of 1776, he was unfortunately delayed in getting to his June meeting. In the meantime the settlers elected him and John Gabriel Jones, a young lawyer, as their representatives—to return to Williamsburg to create the County of Kentucky. (Note 5)

Although George Rogers Clark preferred to negotiate with the Virginia General Assembly for the future status of Kentucky—perhaps as an independent colony, he agreed to do that for which he was elected—create the County of Kentucky from Fincastle County—the western most part of Virginia.

Note 1, Thomas D. Clark, *A history of Kentucky,* (New York, NY, Prentice-Hall, 1937), Page 43.
Note 2, Ibid, Page 43.
Note 3, Ibid, Page 44.
Note 4, Ibid, Page 43.
Note 5, Ibid, Page 45.

George Rogers Clark

CHAPTER 5

The year of 1776 in the American Colonies

In 1776 more settlements continued to spring up in Kentucky. With the relative calm brought about by the peace treaty of Lord Dunmore's War, the settlers were coming to the new Virginia County of Kentucky.

As the Shawnees observed this from across the Ohio River, they saw their great happy hunting ground "Cain-tuc-kee", or "Kain-tuck-e" being ruined by the white settlers. The settler's cows and horses competed with the Indians game for food, and the settlers slaughtered herds of buffalo and elk—for only the tongue, liver, or hide. The white man was also killing Indians—even on their shores north of the Ohio River.

As could be expected, the Shawnee broke the peace treaty, and began to kill the settlers, burn their cabins, steal their horses, and shoot their cattle.

The Shawnees had held a council in Chillicothe, Ohio in 1775 to discuss the nullification of the treaty with Lord Dunmore. With 350 chiefs, sub-chiefs, and thousands of braves, they were ready to wipe out the white settlers from Kentucky—their happy hunting ground.

What a terrible time for George Rogers Clark and the small settlements in Kentucky to ask for help from "Mother Virginia". The war with England was imminent, and Virginia had very little resources to support their goal of independence from an ever increasing taxing King George. They were even less inclined to send troops, money, and supplies to fight for the obscure land of Kentucky—despite the fact that their loyal Virginians were about to be severely threatened by the surging irate Indians.

As mostly everyone knows, the Continent Congress met in Philadelphia, Pennsylvania in July of 1776. After much discussion and some revisions, The Declaration of Independence from England was signed by all thirteen colonies on July 4, 1776—forming the United States of America. Now they would have to fight to make the declaration a reality.

As requested by the Continental Congress of Virginia in 1775, George Rogers Clark and John Gabriel Jones—the duly elected representatives of the settlements of Kentucky showed up in Williamsburg in August of 1776. At this time the Virginia Legislature was naturally beset with British war problems, and had very little time or money to give to the new County of Kentucky. The legislature did finally agree to give George Rogers Clark 500 pounds of gunpowder and lead—to be delivered from Fort Pitt, and to be used to defend the Kentucky area. (Note 1)

As to the request by Clark and Jones to create the County of Kentucky, the legislature said that they would form a committee to consider the matter. Politics in America don't seem to have to changed much in the past 200 plus years.

George Rogers Clark had given another of his persuasive speeches to the Virginia Legislature when asking for supplies and military support for Kentucky. He said, "a territory not worth defending is a territory not worth claiming". His emotional irate speech won over a majority of the Virginia delegates. This speech essentially ended Judge Henderson's claim of his Transylvania Empire. (Note 2)

Anxious to report back to their Kentucky supporters, George Rogers Clark and John Gabriel Jones planed to return by the fastest means available—the Cumberland Gap route. Clark had also written a letter to the settlers at Harrod's Town to arrange to pick up the powder and take it to the Kentucky forts. Just before leaving Williamsburg the two men found out that Clark's letter had not gotten to the settlers, and that the powder and shot was still in Pittsburg. Thus, Clark and Jones set out for Pittsburg in early November of 1776—to get the important supplies themselves. At this time they still did not know if their campaigning for the County of Kentucky had paid off. They would later get some good news—the County of Kentucky was created on December 31, 1776. Thus, George Rogers Clark had earned his title, "The Founder of the Commonwealth of Kentucky". (Note 3)

Note 1, Lowell H. Harrison, *George Rogers Clark and the War in the West,* (Lexington, KY, The University Press of Kentucky, 1976), Page 9.
Note 2, Ibid, Page 9.
Note 3, Ibid, Page 10.

CHAPTER 6
Five Hundred Pounds of Gunpowder and Lead

In early December of 1776, George Rogers Clark and John Gabriel Jones arrived at Fort Pitt. After hiring several men anxious to get to Kentucky, they loaded their valuable cargo onto three canoes. At this point, they realized that the local Indian spies were alerting their allies to follow the white men down the Ohio River. As the Indians ranged closer, Clark under cover of darkness decided to pull into Limestone Creek (near present day Maysville, Kentucky) where he buried the powder and shot in five different places. As a decoy, Clark and Jones stayed on the Kentucky shore and sent their empty canoe down the Ohio River—with the Indians following it. (Note 1)

On December 27, the two men made their way to McClelland's Station—a small outpost in Kentucky. Fortunately the experienced Indian scout Simon Kenton was also at the fort. Since they all knew that the Indians were now very active in Kentucky, Simon recommended that they go south to Harrods Town where they could get a force of at least thirty men to retrieve the gunpowder. To this end George Rogers Clark and Simon Kenton set off to Harrods Town.

After Clark and Kenton left, a headstrong John Gabriel Jones decided to go after the powder himself. With a small force from the station, and no Indian scout, he was soon confronted with a band of Indians under Chief Pluggy. Unfortunately Jones was killed and the fort defeated. When George Rogers Clark and Simon Kenton arrived back from Harrods Town, they found Fort McClellan under siege by the Indians. After a battle, in which Chief Pluggy was killed, the Indians retreated back across the Ohio River. James Harrod and Simon then led a party to retrieve the valuable powder and shot from Three Islands. After five days of zig-zaging to avoid marauding Indians, they delivered the cargo safely to George Rogers Clark's cabin at Harrods Town. (Note 2)

Clark then delivered the life saving powder and shot to all of the remaining forts. The frontiersmen of Kentucky were not free of their Indian nemeses, but they now would live to fight another day—due to the leadership and resourcefulness of George Rogers Clark and his teamwork with James Harrod and Simon Kenton.

Note 1, Lowell H. Harrison, *George Rogers Clark and the War in the West,* (Lexington, KY, The University Press of Kentucky, 1976), Pages 10-11.

Note 2, Thomas D. Clark, *Simon Kenton-Kentucky Scout,* (New York, NY, Farrar & Rinehart, 1943), Pages 121-122.

Chapter 7

Simon Kenton—A. K. A. Simon Butler— The Great Scout

Most great men do not become that way by accident. They are often called brilliant, gifted, lucky, or ordained by God for greatness. Another factor in their equation is that each surrounds themselves with great people for their endeavor. For example, Lewis and Clark had Sacagawea, George Washington had great generals such as Alexander Knox, Nathaniel Greene, Alexander Hamilton, and his young French adventurer—the Marquis De Lafayette. Robert E. Lee had far fewer resources than the North, but had great generals such as Thomas J. "Stonewall" Jackson, J. E. B. Stuart, Jubal Early, and many others. Abe Lincoln finally got it right by promoting U. S. Grant, Sherman, and Sheridan. Ike had great men under him, such as George Patton, Omar Bradley, and admirals "Bull" Halsey and Chester Nimitz.

George Rogers Clark was no exception, in that he found some brave and talented men as his loyal commanders in John Bowman, James Harrod, and Leonard Helm.

Also extremely important for any successful general is the ability to have information about the enemy's location, movements, and size of their force. Before radios, radar, sonar, spy satellites, and cell phones, a commander needed a good scout with a fast horse—or one who was fast on his feet. For example Generals J. E. B. Stuart and Robert E. Lee had a brave and talented scout in John Singleton Mosby. Mosby, as a private often rode near enemy lines and furnished information that helped the South win a number of significant battles. Mosby later became a major, and was the most successful guerilla fighter in the Civil War. Despite all of his many dangerous missions, he lived to be eighty-three years old. (Note 1)

In the case of George Rogers Clark, he was extremely fortunate to find Simon Kenton as a brave, talented, and loyal scout. He accidentally met Simon Kenton at Fort Pitt—the westernmost outpost of America. They learned much from each other while serving in the Kentucky militia during Lord Dunmore's War, and eventually became lifelong friends.

Simon Kenton was the son of a poor hillside Virginia farmer. As a youth he was very lazy and unmotivated to work or go to school. When he became sixteen, he was enamored by a girl named Ellen. She unfortunately thought Simon to be lazy, and not able to support a wife. Along came William Leachman, who was older and a hard worker—a pillar of the community. His marriage to Ellen Cummings was a gala affair—until Simon tried to interrupt the party. Leachman, being older and stronger, gave Simon a beating and sent him limping home. A few days later Simon's father Mark sent him to borrow a saw from William Leachman's new house. Since the saw was nearby in the woods, William went with Simon to get it. When Simon started another fight, William was again beating him unmercifully. Fortunately for Simon, Leachman had long hair. Using his superior brainpower, Simon dragged him to a nearby bramble bush. At this point Simon beat the entangled Leachman until he bled from the nose and mouth. His revenge was complete—but he assumed that Leachman was dead. (Note 2)

In those days killing a man would usually result in a quick hanging for the killer—by the local townspeople—since courthouses and jails were very few. Simon decided to run away to the Ohio valley, where he could be free. For many days he fled west, with very little to eat. He eventually met a fairly well-to-do settler named Butler, who needed a worker for his farm. Simon knew that he would need a gun as he came closer to Indian territory along the Ohio River. Simon asked Mr. Butler if he could work long enough to earn the fine rifle that hung over the door of the cabin. After two weeks of hard work in the fields, the man gave Simon the rifle and better clothes to wear—this time he had been motivated. Simon continued toward the Ohio Valley, confident that he was now free of his past. He did, however, change his name to Simon

Butler in honor of his "cousin Butler"—a name he would carry for nine years. (Note 3)

Simon felt real freedom from his past now, and was not afraid to meet other hunters, traders, and woodsmen. He started to hang out at Fort Pitt on the Ohio River—the last safe outpost for the white man. While there Simon met a man named Yeager who told tales of a great cane land down the Ohio called Kain-tuck-e, where the tall sugar cane grew thickly in thousands of acres.

Simon became obsessed with the idea of seeing the cane and setting up a camp there. He soon met some other men with the same idea. They outfitted a large canoe and started down the Ohio. Soon after their start they met some relatives of Simon's partners—telling them of their father having been captured by Indians. Simon was now left alone forty miles from Fort Pitt, since all of the other men went to aid the captured father. The same thing happened to Simon two more times, once because of winter setting in, and once due to his partners being afraid to go farther—due to Indian sightings. He did finally make it the fourth time—to the mouth of the Kentucky River (present day Carrolton, Kentucky) (Note 4)

Finally, on his fifth try, Simon and a partner made it to his fabled cane land—which he was beginning to believe, did not exist. When he finally made progress up the Kentucky River, Simon was very surprised to see settlements and forts—started by Daniel Boone and James Harrod. He also met his friend from Lord Dunmore's War—George Rogers Clark. Simon Butler made friends quickly with the settlers, and was a great help to defend them from Indian attacks, due to his improving scouting ability and his great marksmanship. (Note 5)

At one point Indians attacked Daniel Boone's fort while Simon and Boone were hunting nearby for food. When Boone was wounded, Simon picked him up and carried him to safety inside the fort. George Rogers Clark was quick to recognize Simon's ability as a scout and a hunter—as first shown during his lead in securing the 500 pounds of powder and shot for the Kentucky settlers. (Note 6)

Note 1, James A. Ramage, *Gray Ghost,* (Lexington, KY, The University Press of Kentucky, 1999), Pages 49-50.

Note 2, Thomas D. Clark, *Simon Kenton—Kentucky Scout,* (New York, NY, Farrar & Rinehart, 1943), Pages 26-27.

Note 3, Ibid, Pages 38-39.

Note 4, Ibid, Page 92.

Note 5, Ibid, Pages 97-98.

Note 6, Ibid, Pages 121-122.

Chapter 8

Secret Orders—For George Rogers Clark's Ears Only

As the Revolutionary War heated up in 1777, the British decided to order Lieutenant Governor Henry Hamilton to their fort in Detroit. His mission was to employ Indians to harass the western Virginia settlements—in order to discourage more colonial settlers to come and form a western independent colony or state. To this end He soon created fifteen war parties of nineteen warriors—each with two British officers as leaders. (Note 1)

It is said that the Indians were given the incentive to join the endeavor by Governor Hamilton paying them in proportion of each white settler's scalp they brought to Detroit. Thus the governor eventually became known as "The Hair Buyer".

In the summer and all of 1777, the Indian attacks became more fierce and more often to threaten the settlements of Harrodsburg and Boonesboro. Realizing the increasing danger to the Kentucky settlers, George Rogers Clark sent two spies to Kaskaskia—a British fort across the Ohio River in the Illinois territory. When they returned in September of 1777, they told Clark that the British had the fort at Kaskaskia well manned, but the town being mostly French, would be friendly toward the American colonists. With this knowledge George Rogers Clark came up with an aggressive plan to attack the British in their claimed territory—thus pushing them and their Indian allies back to Detroit. He also hoped to eventually attack Detroit—the source of the Indian problem. (Note 2)

To this end Clark left for Williamsburg on October 10, 1777, arriving there on December 10. He immediately gave Governor Patrick Henry his plan to attack the British and their Indian allies north of Kentucky and the Ohio River. Although the resources of Virginia were strapped by the Revolutionary War in the east, his argument was convincing. Clark presented the scenario that if the British and Indians are allowed to take over the County of Kentucky, they would soon be attacking the eastern counties of Virginia.

After much debate, George Rogers Clark won over Patrick Henry, Thomas Jefferson, George Mason, and George Wythe to his idea. The Virginia Legislature still needed to approve the plan. But as it was presented to them, it was strictly to provide money and supplies to protect the County of Kentucky. On January 2, 1778 the General Assembly of Virginia authorized the sum of 1,200 pounds for Colonel Clark to defend Kentucky. (Note 3)

Governor Henry soon issued these official orders, for George Rogers Clark to form seven companies of fifty men each from any county of Virginia. With only Patrick Henry, Thomas Jefferson, George Mason, and George Wythe knowing all the facts, they issued a second set of "Secret Orders"—for George Rogers Clark to form as many men as possible to attack the British in Kaskaskia, and as far north as he needed to go in order to wipe out the British threat in the west. (Note 4)

Note 1, Harrison, Lowell H., *George Rogers Clark and the War in the West,*
    Page 11.
Note 2, Ibid, Pages 14-15.
Note 3, Ibid, Page 17.
Note 4, Ibid, Pages 17-18.

CHAPTER 9
Building the Militia in Kentucky

As George Rogers Clark left Williamsburg in January of 1778, he headed northwest across the Appalachian Mountains to Fort Pitt to pick up his authorized supplies and boats for the long trip down the Ohio River. Along the way he recruited some troops, but could not come close to the 350 men (seven companies of fifty) that had been authorized. He camped near Fort Pitt until early May, hoping to pick up more men. He had very little luck recruiting men from Pennsylvania willing to fight for Kentucky. He had been, of course, in competition with recruiters in Virginia looking for men to fight in the eastern part of the Revolution. George Rogers Clark decided that he could wait no longer, and went to Fort Pitt with about 150 men. As Colonel Clark picked up his supplies and boats, he added a few men—but mostly men with families on their way to settle in Kentucky. This would add many women and children to look after. (Note 1)

With George's leadership, and since they were a fairly large force, they had very little trouble from the Indians north of the Ohio River. As they approached the Kentucky River, some of the new settlers wanted to join friends or relatives up the river to Harrodsburg or Boonesboro. George Rogers Clark did unload some salt kettles that were badly needed by the Kentucky settlers. He was, however, very disappointed by getting only a few dozen militia men from the settlements—instead of the 200 he had been promised. (Note 2)

Despite having only half of his promised force, George decided to continue own the Ohio, and make his base on an island—just above the Falls of the Ohio River—where he would later found Louisville,

Kentucky. He and his small militia arrived there on May 27, 1778. Colonel Clark immediately had the troops and the civilians cut trees and build a fort—with blockhouses on the corners to defend it. He also had a few acres cleared and corn planted—thus Corn Island came into being. At Corn Island George Rogers Clark added a few men from the Kentucky settlements, but lost some deserters who found a way to wade to the Kentucky shore. George also created a flat area for his officers to drill his rag-tag troops into a disciplined military force. (Note 3)

At this point only George Rogers Clark knew of the "Secret Orders" to invade the Illinois territory. He soon decided to tell his officers of the plan, and held a council to do so. After much discussion, they agreed to support his plan—although some officers were skeptical of the plan's success.

The next step was to convince his small army to follow this aggressive plan. Fortunately George Rogers Clark had that eloquent persuasive gift of motivation that most great leaders have. He rallied the troops by citing the atrocities that some of the men had witnessed upon their family or friends by savage Indians—most of whom were employed by the British Governor Henry Hamilton of Detroit—known to many as "The Hair Buyer". George convinced most of the troops that this was now their time for revenge!

After the real mission was revealed, a few more men deserted—some to defend their families in the Kentucky settlements. Most were confident in their leader's ability to succeed.

Fortunately George Rogers Clark also had some great officers to rally the militia, namely John Bowman, Leonard Helm, William Harrod (James' brother), and his main expert scout—Simon Kenton. (Note 4)

Note 1, Lowell H. Harrison, *George Rogers Clark and the War in the West,* (Lexington, KY, The University Press of Kentucky, 1976), Pages 19-20.

Note 2, Ibid, Page 20.

Note 3, Ibid, Page 20-21

Note 4, Ibid, Page 21.

Photograph by Douglas C. Harrison

CHAPTER 10

Down the Falls of the Ohio River

In late June of 1778, George Rogers Clark decided that he could wait no longer to start his invasion of the Illinois country—in order to maintain the element of surprise. The Ohio River was also running fairly high, making the trip over the "Falls" somewhat easier. (Note 1)

Fortunately for Colonel Clark, he had his able and loyal scout Simon Kenton, who had been down the Falls of the Ohio. The "Falls" are actually a two and a half mile series of rapids formed by water flowing over a series of limestone ledges, with a drop of only twenty-six feet. The Ohio River meanders from Pittsburg, Pennsylvania to the Mississippi River for a thousand miles. The Mississippi then goes almost another thousand miles to New Orleans, Louisiana. There are no other falls or rapids. Louisville was fortunate to be accidently built as a portage city—at the Falls of the Ohio. (Note 2)

On the morning of June 24, 1778, the small army of 175 men in ten boats made their way a mile above the "Falls", in order to get a straight run at the channel on the west side of the Ohio. With Simon Kenton in the lead boat, the rest followed his lead over the rapids. At this exact time—like a plot from a Hollywood "B" movie—a total eclipse of the sun actually occurred. How strange is that development? Miraculously, in the dark, all of the boats made it over the rapids to a very calm Ohio River. Although a number of the men considered the eclipse to be a bad omen, the invasion into Illinois had begun-inspired by George Rogers Clark's desire to capture Detroit and "The Hair Buyer". His only motivation was to protect his new home in Kentucky, and help America gain its independence from England. (Note 3)

Shortly after Clark left Corn Island for the invasion, two river messengers arrived there with the news that the French had finally signed an alliance with the Colonies. The treaty had been signed on February 16 in Paris, and the news arrived at Corn Island four and a half months later—excellent communication time in 1778. With cell phones and satellite transmission, it would now take about five seconds—how the world has changed! (Note 4)

Realizing the importance of this new development, William Linn, a civilian at Corn Island, hurriedly left by canoe with the precious document. Linn soon delivered the very valuable information to Colonel Clark. Clark was very glad to get this piece of news, and would use it to his advantage to sway the French citizens he would encounter to become American allies. William Linn would stay with Clark and became a valuable officer—eventually becoming a major. (Note 5)

Note 1, Lowell H. Harrison, *George Rogers Clark and the War in the West,* (Lexington, KY, The University Press of Kentucky, 1976), Page 22.

Note 2, George H. Yater, *Two Hundred Years at the Falls of the Ohio,* (Louisville, KY, The Heritage Corporation, 1979), Page 1.

Note 3, Ibid, Pages 4-5.

Note 4, Ibid, Page 5.

Note 5, Ibid, Page5.

Chapter 11

On to the British Fort at Kaskaskia

George Rogers Clark was obsessed with the idea of an invasion of Detroit—the main British outpost in the west during the Revolutionary War. He knew, however, that he first had to secure the British forts at Kaskaskia, and Cahokia on the Mississippi River, and Vincennes on the Wabash River. This was considered necessary in order to limit the flow of supplies to Detroit from the southern rivers.

As the small army went down the Ohio River, they encountered two hunters from Kaskaskia. The men immediately took the oath to fight for America, and to say that Kaskaskia—being made up mostly of French inhabitants—would be friendly toward an American invasion. As the boats neared the mouth of the Ohio River, where it meets the Mississippi River, George Rogers Clark decided to take the one hundred and twenty mile land route—in order to maintain the element of surprise. (Note 1)

The men docked their boats on the north shore of the Ohio, and started the long trek to Kaskaskia, with the new hunter recruits leading the way. After three days their main guide from Kaskaskia, John Saunders got lost, making Colonel Clark suspicious of his loyalty. After threats from Clark, Saunders found the right route to Kaskaskia. After six long days of marching, the tired and hungry army arrived to within a mile west of the town. It was the night of July 4, 1778—how ironic is that? (Note 2)

After obtaining boats, Colonel Clark's army crossed the Kaskaskia River and entered the town. At some time after midnight, they used the element of surprise to open the gates of the fort—and take it over without firing a shot. George Rogers Clark found the Governor Phillip Rocheblave and his wife asleep in bed. After securing the fort

Clark sent most of his troops to take over the town of five hundred, telling the people to stay in their houses or be shot. This was also done without firing a shot, showing the discipline the George Rogers Clark has instilled into his men. (Note 3)

The next morning George Rogers Clark had meetings with the leaders of Kaskaskia, including a Catholic Priest named Father Gibault—who was immediately impressed with Clark's compassion for the French citizens. The people were mostly happy to declare themselves as American citizens, since they were not happy as a British settlement.

The citizens of Kaskaskia had been basically brainwashed by their British leaders to fear the American "Long Knives", stating that they were more fierce than marauding Indians. Once George Rogers Clark told the residents that his men would not rape and pillage like some savages would, their fears were mostly allayed. (Note 4)

He further won their support by revealing the news that King Louis IV of France had become an ally of the United States, and the war might soon be over. (Note 5)

Colonel Clark next sent Governor Rocheblave and his British troops toward Williamsburg with a small garrison escort for the prisoners. He now was ready for his next objective, Cahokia—fifteen miles north and also on the Mississippi River—across from the Spanish settlement of St. Louis.

To this end Clark sent his most trusted commander, Captain John Bowman, and thirty men on horses—loaned by the French citizens of Kaskaskia. He also sent a few Frenchmen to spread the word that the American "Long Knives" were their new best friends. This scenario worked so well that Captain Bowman and his men captured the fort at Cahokia and secured the small towns in between there and Kaskaskia in less than ten days. This was also accomplished without firing a shot. (Note 6)

Note 1, Lowell H. Harrison, *George Rogers Clark and the War in the West,* (Lexington, KY, The University Press of Kentucky, 1976), Page 22.

Note 2, Ibid, Page 23.

Note 3, Ibid, Page 24.

Note 4, Ibid, Page 26.

Note 5, Ibid, Page 27.

Note 6, Ibid, Page 28.

Chapter 12

The British Fort at Vincennes Falls in Line

Just as George Rogers Clark sent Captain Bowman to secure Cahokia, he sent Simon Kenton and two other scouts to check out the British situation in Vincennes. After three nights of spying, while dressed in blankets, and masquerading as Indians, the scouts returned to Kaskaskia. They reported to Colonel Clark that there was no British garrison, and most of the hostile Indians had left also. (Note 1)

At this point George Rogers Clark let it be known that he might call up more troops from Kentucky to help take Vincennes. This, of course, was a total bluff, since no such army existed. Father Gibault and some other leading citizens of Kaskaskia assured Clark that this would not be necessary, and that they would go to Vincennes as friends of the mostly French people there.

The envoys—including one of Clark's men—left for Vincennes on July 14, 1778, armed with only letters to friends and relatives who lived there. The mission was an immediate success. Most of the citizens took the oath of allegiance to America, and a French militia officer unfurled the American flag over Fort Sackville—on the Wabash River at Vincennes. (Note 2)

The envoys and some citizens from Vincennes arrived back in Kaskaskia around the first of August with the good news. At this point George Rogers Clark had captured three major British outposts in less than two months, with a rag-tag army of less than two hundred men, and without a shot being fired. How amazing is that?? He was, however, fortunate in that most people in the area were French, and not happy being occupied by the British.

Because Vincennes was such an important post Colonel Clark sent his most trusted older and mature officer, Captain Leonard Helm to take command of Vincennes—with his headquarters at Fort Sackville. Helm became very helpful in converting many Indian tribes to the French and American side. He would preach Clark's message that the "Long Knives" (or Big Knives) were not invading their territory, but just passing through to defeat the British at Detroit. They used the psychology on the Indians that their French father Louis XVI for whom they fought in the French and Indian War, was glad to have them back as loyal French subjects. Leonard Helm was very effective at conveying this message. (Note 3)

Note 1, Lowell H. Harrison, *George Rogers Clark and the War in the West,* (Lexington, KY, The University Press of Kentucky, 1976), Page 30.

Note 2, Ibid, Page 31.

Note 3, Ibid, Page 31-32.

CHAPTER 13
Indian Treaties at Cahokia

With all of the British forts secure, George Rogers Clark now went to Cahokia in August of 1778 to neutralize the Indian threat in the Illinois Territory. He invited a number of tribes to meet there. Clark would set up a table and place two belts there—a white belt for peace, and a red belt for war. He would give each chief the choice of which belt to take. He would repeatedly use the argument that his army was only passing thru their territory to defeat the British at Detroit. Colonel Clark convinced most of the tribes that the "Great Spirit" was not happy that they left their French father King Louis XVI to fight against him for trinkets and scalps. George Rogers Clark warned the tribes to leave his army a path to Detroit, but if they chose the red belt of war, to fight like men—not squaws. (Note 1)

In five weeks at Cahokia in 1778 Clark signed treaties with at least ten tribes (no tribe took the red belt of war). To follow up these successes, Clark sent agents with each tribe to be sure that they wanted peace.

A modern historian of the frontier concluded, "The great achievement of Clark's 1778 campaign was not the uncontested occupation of the Illinois [Territory], but his success in neutralizing so considerable a segment of the Indian military power upon which English strategy had depended". (Note 2)

Note 1, Lowell H. Harrison, *George Rogers Clark and the War in the West,*
    (Lexington, KY, The University Press of Kentucky, 1976), Pages 31-32.
Note 2, Ibid, Page35.

CHAPTER 14

Party Time in St. Louis

Since the negotiations with the Indians took five weeks—with the many tribes having pow-wows about what to do, one can be sure that George Rogers Clark and his men finally had some leisure time on their hands.

The small Spanish outpost at St. Louis was only two miles across the Mississippi River from Cahokia. The Spanish were fortunately friends of the Americans also, and constant enemies of the British. Although they too were afraid of the savage "Long Knives", the Spanish were convinced by some of their friends that the young commander—George Rogers Clark was civilized. News of his deeds—with no violence had also reached St. Louis.

The Spanish commander, Don Fernando de Leyba invited Clark and his fellow officers to a party with his family in St. Louis. Clark's first visit lasted two days, with he and his men being greeted with an artillery salute, being entertained at a formal dinner, and at dances and late suppers each evening. (Note 1)

Since he stayed at de Leyba's house, tradition has it that George Rogers Clark fell in love with Don Fernando's sister Terese. As things progressed, it is said by some accounts that the two were betrothed. This might explain why Clark never married. It is known, however, that Terese eventually went back to New Orleans, never married, and died in France in 1816 as a nun. (Note 2)

For George Rogers Clark, regardless of his feelings for Terese, he had too much on his plate to have much of a personal life. His sense of duty to the American cause of freedom was his driving force and first priority. As the fall of 1778 approached, Clark needed to return to Kaskaskia to plan for next year's intended conquest of Detroit—to defeat "The Hair Buyer".

Note 1, Lowell H. Harrison, *George Rogers Clark and the War in the West,* (Lexington, KY, 1976), Page 30.
Note 2, Ibid, Page 30.

CHAPTER 15

"The Hair Buyer" Strikes Back

In early August of 1778 a British scout arrived in Detroit. As he broke the news of an American invasion into the Illinois territory, Governor Hamilton became outraged about the situation. He had recently wondered why no Indians had come to Detroit with scalps for rewards, or to bring in prisoners. As Hamilton received the facts that his three outposts had been taken with no casualties, and no shots fired, he no doubt became more upset. After all, he had sent fifteen war parties of well-paid Indians toward the forts that were led by British officers. As he found out, the rebels had only a rag-tag militia, and were led by only a Colonel named Clark. It can be imagined that Governor Hamilton (a. k. a. "The Hair Buyer) blew his stack. (Note 1)

Once Hamilton regained his composure, he started to devise a plan to make the Americans pay for their crimes against the Crown of England. He had been building a force of men and supplies to attack the Americans at Fort Pitt. Governor Hamilton was ordered by his superior officer, General Sir Frederick Haldimand, to divert his effort to regaining his lost outposts—something he wanted to do anyway. (Note 2)

We will never know what would have happened if Hamilton had not been redirected by George Rogers Clark's successful invasions. If George Washington had found it necessary to divert a large part of his struggling army in the fall of 1778 to protect Fort Pitt, he may have suffered many more losses in the eastern part of the war.

Governor Hamilton left Detroit on October 7, 1778 with an army of 245 men—including seventy Indians. He had a large fleet of boats, canoes, and pirogues carrying over 70,000 pounds of supplies. Using the Detroit River, Lake Erie, and the Maumee River, Hamilton soon reached Post Miami (which is present day Fort Wayne). After a short but difficult portage, he reached the Wabash River. By the end of November, Hamilton started to receive information about the American invaders. He knew that a Colonel Clark was at Kaskaskia, and that a Captain Helm was in command at Vincennes. His reports of the number of enemy troops were conflicting, with some informants reporting as many as 280. This is a tribute to Clark's ability to exaggerate his numbers—sometimes by parading the same men around in circles—by going behind a building or a hill. (Note 3)

On December 17, 1778, Governor Hamilton and his army—which now numbered almost six hundred—arrived at Vincennes. They found the American flag flying over Fort Sackville. Captain Helm was still in command, but his French allies had fled, leaving only a handful of men. After scribbling a quick note to Clark about his plight, Captain Helm had no choice but to surrender the fort to Hamilton's overwhelming forces.

Unfortunately the messenger and the note were captured, leaving Colonel Clark with no knowledge of what had happened in December of 1778 in Vincennes. (Note 4)

At Kaskaskia Gorge Rogers Clark had many problems of his own. His supplies and money were getting very low, since he did not take from the French without paying them or using credit, or with his personal I. O. U.'s. He was fortunate in receiving most of his supplies from the friendly Spanish at Saint Louis, and some loyal Americans at New Orleans. At this point Clark was getting no help from Virginia, or the Continental Congress. They were, of course, struggling to finance the Revolution in the east.

Clark had another large problem in that most of his troops three months enlistment period was now over. Of his original force of one hundred and seventy men, he persuaded only one hundred to sign up for another eight months. This was similar to what George Washington had to deal with before his attack on the Hessians at Camden, New Jersey in late December of the same year. Colonel Clark had hoped to regroup and complete his mission to defeat Governor Hamilton at Detroit. What Clark did not know was that his foe was only 145 miles away (as the crow flies), and planning to defeat him—while outnumbering the Americans six to one.

Fortunately for George Rogers Clark, Governor Hamilton decided to stay in Vincennes for the winter, and improve the defenses of Fort Sackville. At this point with a much greater advantage, Governor Hamilton decided to procrastinate—spring would be a much better time to rout the invaders. This decision led to his downfall. He justified the delay since the weather was bad and his troops were worn out from their six hundred mile trip from Detroit in seventy-one days. In mid December of 1778, Governor Hamilton's force of near six hundred dwindled to some ninety-six men by the end of January 1779. He was not concerned since all of his men had orders to return in the spring. (Note 5)

Hamilton apparently became so relaxed that he became friends with his personable prisoner Captain Helm. It is said that the two men spent much time together—trading stories, barbs, and drinking toddies that Helm would make.

Note 1, Lowell H. Harrison, *George Rogers Clark and the War in the West,* (Lexington, KY, The University Press of Ky), Pg 39-40.
Note 2, Ibid, Pg 40.
Note 3, Ibid, Pg 41-42.
Note 4, Ibid, Pg 42-43,
Note 5, Ibid, Page 44.

CHAPTER 16

George Rogers Clark Wades Back to Vincennes

With no reliable information from Vincennes or Detroit, George Rogers Clark spent an uneasy January of 1779 in Kaskaskia. There were rumors that Governor Hamilton had left Detroit, and that British Soldiers and hostile Indians were in the area, but no skirmishes occurred.

On January 29 Clark finally got some accurate information about the status of Vincennes from Frances Vigo—a Spanish merchant from St. Louis (a county in Indiana near Terre Haute is named for him). Vigo had been arrested by a British patrol on his way to Vincennes to arrange for provisions and ammunition for Captain Helm at Fort Sackville. He was soon released since he was a Spanish citizen, and theoretically neutral. There is an unconfirmed story that Hamilton made Vigo promise to not give the Americans any information about the British on his trip home. It is said that Vigo obeyed his promise and went straight to St. Louis. He then hurried to Kaskaskia to give his friend George Rogers Clark all of the information he had learned while a captive at Vincennes. (Note 1)

After learning the facts about Vincennes from Vigo, Clark had a grave decision to make—to attack "The Hair Buyer" now or wait until spring. At this point in time Clark knew that Hamilton would be most vulnerable. If he waited until spring, he might be hopelessly outnumbered. Clark also worried that Hamilton would follow his retreat back to the Falls of the Ohio, and wipe out the struggling settlements in Kentucky. Thus Clark decided that he must attack the British now—despite the winter weather, and the possible flooding of the many rivers between Kaskaskia and Vincennes.

Having made the decision to attack the British at Vincennes, Clark hurriedly made preparations for the raid. He recruited some French citizens and got some mules as pack animals to carry their supplies. He also bought a boat that he called the *Willing*, and equipped it with supplies, cannons, and over forty men. The captain was John Rogers—his cousin on his mother's side. The *Willing* left on February 5, 1779 to go a circuitous route to cut off any southern escape by Hamilton. It would go down the Kaskaskia River to the Mississippi River, then south to the Ohio, and finally up the Wabash to help attack Fort Sackville at Vincennes. (Note 2)

George Rogers Clark left Kaskaskia the next afternoon with a force of 170 men—the same number that he had when leaving the Falls of the Ohio. At this juncture, however, more than half of his men were French. The men did not realize that they had to travel 180 miles of mostly flooded country.

The first six days of the trip went well, with the pack horses carrying most of the gear, and game plentiful for food. The army had averaged over twenty-five miles per day, leaving them less than ten miles from Vincennes.

The bad news came soon when they reached the Little Wabash River on February 13. Although normally separated from the Wabash River by three miles, the two rivers had merged into one great five mile expanse of water—by the heavy rains and melting snow. One can imagine that there were many expletives spoken by Clark and his men at this time. (Note 3)

Much of the almost five mile wide wall of water was only two or three deep, buy many areas were much deeper. Clark hastily had a pirogue (a large canoe) made from nearby trees. The men used the boat to find the shallowest areas to wade through. Once across the Little Wabash, they built scaffolding for themselves and their supplies. Another small stream was crossed on the following day, and the men made camp on some fairly high ground. The pirogue again came in very handy to carry supplies—and those men too ill to walk. Their small drummer boy helped to keep the men's morale fairly high by floating across the rivers and streams on his drum. (Note 4)

On February 17 the little army was less than ten miles from Vincennes—so close that they could hear the morning cannon from Fort Sackville. They were now near the Embarass and Wabash Rivers. The men waded about, hoping to find a shallow place to cross the Wabash River. They had no luck, but did find a piece of muddy high ground on which to camp. At this point Clark and his men were wet, cold, tired, and very hungry. They were hoping to soon see their ship the *Willing* sail up the Wabash with food, supplies, and a way to cross the swollen river. Unfortunately the ship had been delayed by fighting the strong downstream current.

After two more days with no food and no boat showing up, the men were very demoralized—with the French volunteers talking about going back home. Luckily the army's river guard soon captured a boat from Vincennes and five French hunters—who immediately became friendly to the Americans (the French tended to co-operate with whoever is in charge of their towns and their lives). One of the French hunters had killed a deer, which was soon shared by Clark and his men. The Frenchmen also volunteered the information that Fort Sackville was now lightly defended, and no one knew an American army was nearby. (Note 5)

George Rogers Clark now decided that he could no longer wait for the *Willing,* and ordered the men to build two canoes to ferry his troops across the Wabash River

On the morning of February 21, Clark ordered the men to use the two canoes to do the ferrying. This was finally completed, and the troops reassembled on a hill five miles from Vincennes. Clark had hoped to reach the town that day. But after another three miles of marching—mostly through water with some of it shoulder high—he knew that they must camp again, and found a muddy hill.

The small wet and tired army pushed on the next day, reaching a plain nearly four miles wide that had become flooded into a lake. After assuring the men that they would be able to see Vincennes after reaching the woods across the lake, George Rogers Clark plunged into the chilly water up to his chest. Despite their weakened condition, all of the troops made the crossing. The strong men helped the weaker ones, and some were put into the canoes. It is amazing that no one drowned, and that they were able to keep their rifles dry by holding them above their heads. Unfortunately the men found the woods still flooded, and had to continue on to find dry land. (Note 6)

Then, some might say—a miracle occurred. The men captured a canoe carrying Indian women and children. It was loaded with food—a half quarter of buffalo, corn, and some tallow. The men found a woods called Warriors Island. After building fires, drying themselves off, and feeding themselves, their morale soared. From the far edge of the woods, they could see their target—Vincennes and Fort Sackville. (Note 7)

Note 1, Lowell H. Harrison, *George Rogers Clark and the War in the West,* (Lexington, KY, The University Press of Kentucky), Pg 47.
Note 2, Ibid, Page 48. Note 3, Ibid, Page 49. Note 4, Ibid, Page 50.
Note 5, Ibid, Page 52. Note 6, Ibid, Page 53-54. Note 7, Ibid, Page 54.

CHAPTER 17

George Rogers Clark Captures "The Hair Buyer"

Recapturing Fort Sackville at Vincennes for the second time would not be as easy as the first. Clark did not even go the first time in 1778. He sent only a few men under Captain Helm and some French allies—including their new best friend—Father Pierre Gibault.

This time in Vincennes, Clark did as he had done in Kaskaskia—he sent the French residents he had captured into town to tell the other citizens to stay in their houses to avoid being killed. They were told that they could also go to Fort Sackville—if they wanted to defend it with the British (none of the French citizens did). Although Governor Hamilton had sent out scouts to check out the nearby campfires, he was not concerned about any organized attacks. He was not even alarmed by the lack of French citizens on the streets of Vincennes. (Note 1)

As Clark's main force occupied the town, he sent fifteen men to fire at the fort as evening approached on February 22. Governor Hamilton assumed that the shots came from marauding Indians. One legend has it that Captain Helm, the main prisoner of "The Hair Buyer" came to see him shortly before any shots were fired. The two had apparently become friendly enemies during the mostly boring winter downtime. It is said that Captain Helm complimented Governor Hamilton on the many improvements he had done to the fort. He then told Hamilton in his Kentucky country dialect: "It's a shame ye aint gonna get to keep it".

Once a number of Hamilton's men were killed and wounded by Clark's Kentucky long rifles, the Governor ordered his men to man their arms and cannons to defend the fort—finally realizing that this was really an enemy attack. (Note 2)

At about the same time Clark received some much needed gunpowder from the French. He was also approached by the Indian chief Tobacco's Son who had become a "big knife" back in Cahokia (pledging to be an ally of the Americans against the British). Tobacco's Son volunteered his one hundred braves to help George Rogers Clark attack Fort Sackville. After careful consideration, Clark very diplomatically declined the chief's offer—fearing that his men might confuse them for hostile Indians. (Note 3)

In another brilliant move Clark realized that the cannons of the fort could not fire very low. They were mainly set up to defend the nearby Wabash River. If Clark's ship the *Willing* had arrived, a major cannon battle would have erupted—probably with the Americans on the losing side. Clark soon built breastworks for his men to take cover behind, and fire at the fort at close range. As Hamilton's men would light the fuse to fire their ineffective canons, Clark's Kentucky sharpshooters would kill or wound them by shooting through the gunports. Although a couple of Clark's men were wounded (the first casualties since they had left the Falls of the Ohio), the cannons were soon silenced. This type of assault continued through the next day—February 23. (Note 4)

Knowing that he had Hamilton overwhelmed, George Rogers Clark demanded his surrender on the morning of February 24th. George Rogers Clark and Governor Henry Hamilton finally met—at a Catholic church in Vincennes. With typical British pride, Hamilton did not accept the terms of surrender—saying he would fight off any siege by the Americans. On the next morning, however, Governor Hamilton reconsidered, and surrendered Fort Sackville and Vincennes unconditionally to Colonel George Rogers Clark—on February 25, 1779. "The Hair Buyer" and twenty-four of his troops were soon shackled in chains, and prepared to be sent through Kentucky to Williamsburg as prisoners of war. (Note 5)

Clark's "battleship" the *Willing* finally arrived on February 27, too late for action, but was very useful to return troops and prisoners back to Kentucky.

Note 1, Lowell H. Harrison, *George Rogers Clark and the War in the West*, (Lexington, KY, The University Press of Kentucky), Pages 55-56.
Note 2, Ibid, Page 56.
Note 3, Ibid, Page56.
Note 4, Ibid, Pages 56-57.
Note 5, Ibid, Pages 59-60.

Monument to George Rogers Clark at Vincennes, Indiana-Photograph by
Douglas C. Harrison

CHAPTER 18

George Washington uses Clark's Victories to Boost Morale

When George Washington found out about George Rogers Clark's incredible victory in Vincennes, he was elated. Since morale was very low during the winter of 1779 in the east, a major victory against the British anywhere was a great morale booster.

We will never know how many troops the British had to send to Detroit to re-man their outpost. Washington was also very pleased that Clark had accomplished so much with no help from the Continental Congress, since he was having a very tough time getting funds for his own under-equipped army. In any case, the Revolutionary War in the west was virtually over—at least allowing George Washington to totally concentrate his attention to the main part of the war.

CHAPTER 19
George Rogers Clark Returns to Kentucky

With the three main forts in the Illinois territory under his control, and most of the Indians subdued or taken on as allies, George Rogers Clark decided to return to Kentucky—in the summer of 1779. Since most of his mens' enlistment time was over, Clark knew that an invasion of Detroit was currently out of the question.

Knowing that Corn Island might eventually be under water, and was too small to hold the flood of incoming settlers, Clark had designed a fort to be built just above the island—in order to protect them better and avoid flooding. To this end, in the summer of 1778, Clark had sent Captain William Linn (the hero of giving Clark the French ally news) to supervise the construction. The fort was occupied in the fall of 1779 at what is now 12th and Rowan streets near present downtown Louisville, Kentucky.

After leaving a garrison of soldiers at Kaskaskia, Cahokia, and Vincennes, Clark left for the Falls of the Ohio with the rest of the troops. He arrived at his yet unnamed settlement on August 20, 1779—having been gone for fourteen months. Fortunately Clark and his men had a "home" to come back to, due to his foresight. The plan of his new fort consisted of cabins, blockhouses on the corners to fight off enemies, and stockades for prisoners. A few of the cabins had puncheon floors (split logs laid with the level side up), but most were tamped dirt. (Note 1)

Apparently George Rogers Clark was so pleased with the fort that he wanted to show it off, and celebrate his victories in Illinois. To this end he invited settlers from Fort Harrod and Logans fort to feast with him. Clark had rum and sugar brought from Kaskaskia—and perhaps some French wine. He also had a puncheon floor built at a larger cabin (called Bachelor's Hall) for dancing. Fifteen men and three women came from the other forts—despite the sighting of Indians along the way. The dancing was lively, and most likely done to fiddle playing—the most common musical instrument of the day. One can imagine that George Rogers Clark now had time to reminisce about his partying days in St. Louis, and dancing with the lovely senorita—Teresa de Leyba. The dance floor at the fort was far less elegant, but the party apparently went on or several days. It was the social event of the year at the Falls of the Ohio in 1779. (Note 2)

Although various monuments have been erected at the site of the fort, vandals destroyed them all. The location is still alive with activity. It is now the headquarters of Mercer Transportation, Inc., a large trucking company owned by local entrepreneur James Lee Stone. Fittingly perhaps, the site is now the permanent home of an eight hundred pound steel structure in the shape of a cross. Mercer Transportation had helped to clear the wreckage of the 911 site, and brought the structure to their headquarters as a tribute to those who perished in that tragic event.

The fort at 12th and Rowan was only occupied for four years during the Revolutionary War. It never had an official name, but was sometimes called "The White Fort". With more settlers coming in, it soon became necessary to build a larger fort up river—above the Falls of the Ohio, and nearer to where the settlers were building cabins.

Note 1, George H. Yater, *Two Hundred Years at the Falls of the Ohio*, (Louisville, KY, The Heritage Corp., 1979), Page 6. Note 2, Ibid, Page 10.

CHAPTER 20

Louisville Becomes a City

In late 1779, George Rogers Clark had more time to concentrate on the city that he had accidently founded at Corn Island in 1778. He was very pleased with the French King Louis XVI having become an ally—and giving him a great propaganda tool to help take over the British controlled, but mainly French towns. To this end Clark sent a message to the settlers he had left at Corn Island. He told them to name their little settlement "Lewisville" in honor of their new ally. Spelling and punctuation were not Clark's strong suit. Now that he was at home in his founded town, George Rogers Clark made the first detailed map of Louisville in 1779. His vision for streets and forts were the foundation of Louisville. (Note 1)

Unfortunately for Clark, three hundred families came down the Ohio in1779 and settled in Louisville. The winter was very harsh, and the people and the town barely survived. The British and Indian problem arose again in 1780. Although George Rogers Clark led more raids to protect Louisville and the Kentucky settlements, he never had the troops needed to attack Detroit, and totally eliminate the British and Indians from Kentucky.

At this point in time, Clark had to spend all of his time and energy trying to pay off the personal debts he had incurred to finance the Revolutionary War in the west. He basically spent the rest of his life trying to get money from Virginia and the Continental Congress.

At least George Rogers Clark had the pleasure of seeing the little settlement he had started become an official city on May 1, 1780, having been approved by the Government Assembly of Virginia. (Note 2)

Despite many of the new settlers of Louisville wanting to run the town, Clark still had the best vision of how to defend the new settlement. The British and Indians were still a threat nearby.

Clark realized the need for another fort to the east—where most of the settlers had moved. To this end he built a larger somewhat medieval fort at Seventh Street where the B & O Railroad station was eventually located. This fort was called Fort Nelson and was completed in 1782. The fort was surrounded by an eight foot wide moat. (Note 3)

With his financial problems mounting, George Rogers Clark soon retired to a small cabin across the Ohio River—with his fame and fortune days over at the ripe old age of twenty-nine. Fortunately George Rogers Clark had a large family—ready to support his accomplishments. He had basically won the vast Northwest Territory for America—consisting of the current states of Indiana, Illinois, Ohio, Wisconsin, and Michigan.

Note 1, R. C. Riebel, *Louisville Panorama,* (Louisville, KY, Liberty National Bank and Trust Company of Louisville, 1954), Page 10.

Note 2, Ibid, Page 21.

Note 3, Ibid, Page 19.

CHAPTER 21

The Clarks of Virginia

While George Rogers Clark was busy in the west from 1779 to 1782 defending and building Louisville, three of his five brothers were fighting the Revolution in the east.

Jonathan the oldest brother was a captain with George Washington at Valley Forge. He fought bravely in a number of battles, including The Battle of Monmouth in 1778 (the first real American victory), and eventually became a general.

John Clark, or Johnny as he was called, was a captain in the Continental Army. Unfortunately he was captured with many others, when the Americans lost The Battle of Brandywine in 1777. He spent the rest of the war on a British prison ship, and died at age twenty-six—probably of tuberculosis.

Lieutenant Edmund Clark fought in the siege of Charles Town (now Charleston) South Carolina in 1780. Although all of the Clark sons became expert riflemen, Edmund was apparently the best. It was said that he could shoot the head from a turkey at a distance of one hundred yards. Unfortunately, at the siege of Charles Town, he never got to fire a shot. He was forced to surrender along with all of the American troops after a long siege. The Rebels were outnumbered ten to one. Edmund was later released in a prisoner exchange.

Richard Clark, at age nineteen, was finally allowed by father John Clark to join big brother George at Kaskaskia in the summer of 1779. Since Vincennes had been won that February, Richard—as a private—did not see any military action. In the Continental Army, as in most armies, enlisted men and officers can not socialize. Thus George

Rogers Clark promoted his brother to lieutenant—so they could drink together—another case of its not what you know, but who you know.

Back at the Clark plantation in Virginia in the summer of 1779, father John, mother Ann Rogers, sisters Ann, Lucy, Elizabeth, and little brother Billy were busy growing extra crops to support the war effort. Frances Eleanor Clark (Fanny), the tenth and last child of John and Ann Rogers Clark was only six at this time. Billy, the ninth child was eight years old and growing up quickly. He could do many chores and work in the fields. His brother Edmund had already taught William how to load and shoot a rifle.

At this point in time only George Rogers Clark had become a Kentuckian. The rest of this great family was still "The Clarks of Virginia". It is amazing that the bulk of the family would eventually leave their large plantation, and move the relatively unsettled County of Kentucky.

This again shows the persuasive powers of George Rogers Clark. He, of course, had arranged for large tracts of fertile land for them that he had surveyed near Louisville. One would also assume that the plantation in Virginia was becoming much less productive—due to no rotation of crops. This fact would most likely make their decision to move easier.

After the war in 1784, George's father John, mother Ann Rogers, sisters Lucy, Elizabeth, Frances (Fanny), brothers Jonathan, Edmund, and William all moved to Louisville—thus forming the foundation of "The Clarks of Kentucky". Ann Clark would stay in Virginia and marry Owen Gwathmey. They would also eventually move to Kentucky with their eleven children.

GENEOLOGY OF THE CLARKS OF KENTUCKY

John Clark	MARRIED	Ann Rogers
	.	
Jonathan Clark— Aug 7, 1750	.	
	.	
GEORGE ROGERS CLARK—	.	

Nov 19, 1752-Feb. 13, 1818   '

'

Ann Clark (Gwathmey)—   '
July 19, 1752

John Clark—Sept 15, 1757   '

Richard Clark—July 6, 1760   '

.

Edmund Clark—   '
Sept. 25, 1762

Lucy Clark (Croghan)—   '
Sept 15, 1765

Eliz. Clark (Anderson)—   '
Feb 11, 1768

.

Frances Eleanor Clark—   .
Jan. 20, 1773

.

WILLIAM CLARK—   MARRIED   Julia Hancock.
Aug 1, 1770
-Sept. 1, 1838   .

'

MERIWETHER LEWIS   .
CLARK, Sr.
—Jan 10, 1809-Oct. 28,   MARRIED   Abigail Churchill
1881

'

MERIWETHER LEWIS
Clark, Jr.
—Jan. 27, 1846-Apr. 22,
1899.

CHAPTER 22

Little Brother Billy Grows Up

As great as George Rogers Clark's victories were in helping to win the Revolutionary War in the west, his great career was basically over by the time he was thirty years old. William (or Billy as he was called by the family as a youngster) was only thirteen at this point. Billy had become a worshiper of his big brother, as George would briefly come home to the family plantation in Albemarle County, Virginia—on each of his three trips to Williamsburg.

On George's first trip home from Kentucky, Billy was only three years old—there being a seventeen year difference in their ages. All of the family members were fascinated by George's stories about the Indians, the British, and the vast areas of fertile land in Kentucky.

William quickly became the number one fan of big brother George. As he grew up, William vowed to become a hero like George. Having been born in 1770, he was too young to join his five brothers in the Revolutionary War—since it was basically over in 1783.

With the war over, George and Jonathan Clark started to build a large two story cabin on 300 acres that George had surveyed and claimed for his parents. Being on a hill in nearby Louisville, Kentucky, and surrounded by Mulberry trees, they named it Mulberry Hill. They planned to have the house finished, furnished, and provisioned by late 1784.

Thus John and Ann Rogers Clark, and all of the unmarried children living at home, left their large stone house in Virginia for a log cabin in Kentucky. They left in late October, hoping to spend Christmas in their new home. All of their belongings were loaded into three covered wagons—John and Ann Rogers Clark leading the way.

Edmund (age 22), and William (age 14) drove the other two wagons. Sisters Lucy (age 19), Elizabeth (age 16), and Fanny (age 11), and eight slaves—including York, Cupid, Venus, and Old Rose made up the rest of the group.

William was maturing quickly, and began to show his leadership abilities on the trip. The convoy followed the Potomac River northwest to Fort Cumberland (present day Cumberland, Maryland). They then headed northwest, crossing the Allegheny Mountains, and hoping to go by boat on the Monongahela River to Pittsburg, and then by boat to their new home in Kentucky for Christmas.

Unfortunately for the Clark caravan, winter set in early in 1784. The Alleghenies were covered with deep snow as they descended. William took over to lead the wagon train by holding the bridle of the lead horse, and walking slowly through the snow to follow the narrow path down the mountain.

When the wagons reached the Monongahela River, they found a Captain Greathouse with flatboats to rent—also bound for the Falls of the Ohio. After selling the wagons—but keeping three horses—the Clarks loaded their possessions onto their rented flatboat. Unfortunately the river soon froze solid, making it impossible to move by water.

CHAPTER 23
The Clarks of Redstone Fort

When the beleagured Clark family arrived at nearby Redstone Fort on the frozen Monongahela River, they were relieved to have a place to stay, but disappointed that they would not make it to Kentucky for Christmas. They also found out that ice was forming on the nearby Ohio River. The Clarks became resolved to spending the winter of 1884-1885 at Redstone Fort. John and Ann Rogers Clark yearned to see George, and their young son Richard, who had joined George after the last Vincennes campaign. William going on fifteen was maturing rapidly, and was anxious to go with George on some of his trips as Head Indian Commissioner. This would now all have to wait until spring. (Note 1)

As the winter of 1785 dragged on at Redstone Fort, the Clark family kept themselves fairly busy. The men went hunting and planned for the trip south. The women kept busy cooking and mending clothes. William started to work with Mr. Greathouse's men to learn how to navigate the winding Ohio River, and how to steer the tiller bar on the large flatboat that would take them to Kentucky.

A flatboat or "Kentucky Boat" was easily constructed to float down the Ohio River. It was made of large wooden planks, and was basically an oversized raft. The boats were often eighteen feet wide and forty feet long, with a cabin for shelter. As naturalist John James Audubon describes it, the boat contained men, women, and children huddled together, with horses, cattle, and poultry. The deck of the boat was like a farmyard, containing hay and various farming equipment. (Note 2)

It is amazing that cattle, skittish horses, and other animals could survive such a journey—and not cause leaks in the boat, or jump overboard. The boats did have high sides—probably for that reason. The high sides were also for protection from Indian attacks.

Another reason for the boats to be made of thick planks—the boat would be disassembled, and the planks sold for a good profit in Louisville. The planks were in demand to be used to build houses—which quickly became more prestigious than log cabins. It was into this flatboat environment that the Clark family was about to trust their lives and possessions.

Note 1, Kathleen Jennings, *Louisville's First Families: a Series of Genealogical Sketches,* (Louisville, KY, The Standard Printing Co., 1920), Pages 45-46.

Note 2, George H. Yater, *Two Hundred Years at the Falls of the Ohio,* (Louisville, KY, The Heritage Corporation, 1979), Page 19.

CHAPTER 24

Finally—The Clarks of Kentucky

In February of 1785, the ice on the Monongahela and nearby Ohio Rivers began to break up. Mr. Greathouse was also anxious to get to Louisville, and the Clark family loaded the balance of their goods that it had been necessary to use at Redstone Fort during the winter.

They were finally on their way again following the Monongahela River. Soon they could see the Alleghany River coming in from the north, the growing town of Pittsburg, and Fort Pitt—where the two rivers would join to form the Ohio River. The Clarks were now only six hundred and seven winding river miles from their new Kentucky home.

After stopping at Fort Pitt for more supplies the boats started down the Ohio. They were soon joined by other settlers headed for Kentucky. They soon arrived at Wheeling (now West Virginia), and stopped at a fort that George Rogers Clark had built. At this point the Clark's boat was joined by more settlers, making up a flotilla of approximately twelve boats.

The threat of Indian attacks was still present, although somewhat less—due to the British surrender at Yorktown in October of 1783. The boats stayed in the middle of the Ohio River—to avoid roving bands of Indians on the Indiana side, and hunting parties on the Kentucky side. They soon passed a place called Grave Crick, where George had first settled while he was first surveying in Kentucky. They were soon to pass a number of inlets on the Indiana side of the Ohio where George had fought Indians.

As February turned into March, the flotilla made it to the mouth of the Kentucky River. Some of the boats at this point left to join friends and relatives at Harrodsburg and Boonesboro about fifty miles up the river. George also might also have made his final home near Harrodsburg, since he had lived there for a number of years. There might never have been a Louisville if George had not decided to launch his attack on British forces from the Falls of the Ohio.

While stopping at this location on March 3, 1785, John Clark went to visit the cabin of a friend he had known in Virginia, a Captain Elliot—on the north side of the Kentucky River (near present day Carrolton, Kentucky). With the captain away hunting, his wife did not invite John Clark in, or ask his party to stay overnight nearby—apparently due to her being ashamed of their humble cabin. John Clark immediately left and his group continued down the Ohio. Ironically the Elliot cabin was very soon attacked and Mrs. Elliot's brother killed and the cabin set on fire. Mrs. Elliot and her daughter escaped down to the river, and hid from them until Captain Elliot returned. The Clarks had dodged the bullet, as the saying goes—or in this case dodged the arrows and the fire. (Note 1)

Not knowing about the problem at the mouth of the Kentucky, the rest of the Clark entourage continued down the Ohio. After one more night's stopover, the Clarks could hear the Falls of the Ohio—meaning that they were only five or so miles from Louisville. They finally arrived at Fort Nelson on March 15, 1785. John, Ann Rogers, Lucy, Elizabeth, William, and Fanny now joined George as the Clarks of Kentucky.

Note 1: Kathleen Jennings, *Louisville's First Families: a Series of Genealogical Sketches,* (Louisville, KY, The Standard Printing Co., 1920), Page 46.

Chapter 25

The Clarks Find Their Thrill—on Mulberry Hill

The Clark family was soon taken by wagons to their new home southeast of Louisville, on a hill near Beargrass Creek. As they saw their new three hundred acre plantation, they were thrilled by the large mulberry and locust trees, the fertile soil, and the handsome two-story log cabin that Jonathan and George had built for them. The house was probably one of the largest in Louisville at the time—measuring twenty feet by forty feet, and consisting of many rooms. There was also a detached one story kitchen, and cabins for the Clark's slaves. One report states the house was built using mulberry logs. (Note 1)

As the family settled into their new home, George Rogers Clark returned from a trip as Indian Commissioner. He was thrilled to see his family in their new setting—the Clarks of Kentucky. He was also thrilled to again have his own room where he could study, invent, or write letters to Congress for reimbursement of the great sums of money owed to him.

William, soon to be fifteen, was thrilled to have his big brother—the hero of the west—near so he could hear new stories of George's adventures. Lucy was thrilled to be near brother George's surveying partner that she had met—Bill Croghan (pronounced Crawn). The rest of the Clark family was thrilled to quickly become prominent in the Louisville community—due mostly to George's leadership in the area.

As the Clark family continued to settle into their new home in 1885, life was pleasing for the most part, except for the occasional

Indian threat. John and Ann Rogers were very busy running their new plantation. The three girls were enjoying their new life, while breaking into Louisville society—such as it was. The attractive young Clark women were, of course, being called upon by numerous suitors from Louisville.

In this era horses or a horse and wagon, or carriage were the only means of transportation between Louisville and Mulberry Hill. Never in their wildest dreams could the Clark women have envisioned a Louisville series of social events also centered around horses but about thoroughbred horses racing. This event to be started by their great uncle to be—Meriwether Lewis Clark, Jr., and at a famous race track less than three miles from Mulberry Hill.

George was very happy to now have the support of most of his large family, but his financial problems were mounting. A great diversion for him was to be able to teach William how to survey and make maps—knowledge he would unknowingly need in the future.

Note 1, Kathleen Jennings, *Louisville's First Families: a Series of Genealogical Sketches,* (Louisville, KY, The Standard Printing Co., 1920), Page 47.

CHAPTER 26
George Rogers Clark's Last Indian Fight

In January of 1786, William went with George to a council with some Indian tribes at the mouth of the Miami River (near present day Cincinnati, Ohio). Although a peace treaty was signed, it was soon violated by the warlike Shawnee Indians. Why a prominent high school in Louisville was named for them is very ironic.

Later in 1786 George was selected to lead a raid against waring Indians in towns on the Wabash River. With drafted men, who had no heart to fight, lacking supplies, and some men that mutinied, Clark had no choice but to withdraw without a victory. He did negotiate a cease fire with the Indians—mostly due to his great ability to bluff—again making his forces sound much larger than reality. (Note 1)

Unfortunately for George, other men now hungry for power in the new valuable territory were trying to ruin his reputation. A foppish and conniving former Revolutionary War general from Lexington named James Wilkinson spread rumors that Clark was drunk on duty during the Wabash raid. This led to Clark's removal as Indian Commissioner and guess who later got he job—James Wilkinson. Although George fought the rumors, his reputation was only restored many years later. (Note 2)

Note 1, Lowell H. Harrison, *George Rogers Clark and the War in the West,* (Lexington, KY, The University Press of Kentucky, 1976), Pages102-103.
Note 2, Ibid, Page 104.

CHAPTER 27
More Clark relatives to Come

From 1786 to 1789 life was good for the Clark family at Mulberry Hill. Except for George's continuing problems, everyone was doing well. Elizabeth married Colonel Richard Anderson in August of 1787, and was soon adding to the family. Lucy married her long time beau Major William (Bill) Croghan on July 18, 1789. They too would eventually add eight children to the Clark clan. Jonathan would eventually move to Kentucky in 1802, and add his seven children to the tribe. Ann Clark and Owen Gwathmey, not to be outdone had eleven children and moved to Louisville in 1800. Brother Edmund also moved to Louisville in 1803, but never married. (Note 1)

Unfortunately John and Richard would also have no offsprings—due to their being deceased as young men. George was driven to other agendas and had little time for courting. There are some accounts that say that George hoped to marry his Spanish lady from St. Louis, Teresa de Leyba. In those violent and changing times it never did work out. William at nineteen years of age in 1789 would do his important part later.

Note 1, Kathleen Jennings, *Louisville's First Families: a Series of Genealogical Sketches,* (Louisville, KY, The Standard Printing Co., 1920), Pages 48-54.

Chapter 28

William Clark Becomes a Soldier

With the threat of Indians still present in 1789, William Clark at age nineteen joined the Kentucky Militia as an ensign—to help to defend his new home. Since big brother George could no longer serve as an effective leader, William apparently felt it was his duty to continue the family tradition.

That year William traveled with Major John Hardin up the Wabash River to attack the Wea Indians—who had been raiding settlements in Kentucky. Unfortunately the inexperienced force attacked a peaceful Shawnee hunting party, which added to the rift between the Kentuckians and the Shawnee Indians. (Note 1)

In 1790 William Clark was commissioned as a captain in the Clarksville militia by General Arthur St. Clair, the governor of the Northwest Territory. This would seem rather fitting, since William's brother George had greatly helped to win this vast territory for America during the Revolutionary War. William was soon sent on a number of scouting missions for the governor. This fortunately kept him out of the disastrous Indian fight in the Northwest Territory—led by the inept General Josiah Harmar. (Note 2)

After losing more battles to the Indians north of the Ohio River, George Washington called upon one of his Revolutionary War heroes to fight the Indians—General "Mad" Anthony Wayne.

William Clark finally joined the regular army as a lieutenant on March 6, 1792, and was assigned to General Wayne. His commission was signed by none other than President Washington—perhaps as a tribute to the other Clark brothers who had served nobly during the Revolution—Jonathan, John, George, Edmund, and Richard. (Note 3)

William Clark was involved in a number of skirmishes with Indians, and was thanked by General Wayne for his good conduct during the fight. William fought gallantly at the Battle of Fallen Timbers in 1794, by commanding a company of riflemen—which drove the enemy back on the left flank—and helped to win the battle. (Note 4)

Note 1, William Clark (explorer)—Wikipedia, the free encyclopedia, Page 2.
Note 2, Ibid, Page 2.
Note 3, Ibid, Page 2.
Note 4, Ibid, Page 2.

CHAPTER 29

Enter Meriwether Lewis—the Hothead

Meriwether Lewis grew up in Charlottesville, Virginia as part of the landed gentry. His mother and father were both from prominent Virginia families. Their plantation was only eight miles from Monticello, where their famous neighbor lived—Thomas Jefferson.

Meriwether Lewis was born on August 18, 1774. His father William being a patriot, joined the Revolution when war broke out in 1775. He served without pay, and paid his own expenses. William unfortunately died of pneumonia in 1779—a result of almost drowning while crossing a flooded river. Thus, Meriwether Lewis barely knew his father. Fortunately Lewis' mother Lucy remarried a well-to-do planter—Captain John Marks, who apparently treated his step-son well. Meriwether was able to grow up as a Virginia gentleman—being educated and associating with Virginia society figures including the family friend—Thomas Jefferson. (Note 1)

Meriwether Lewis was anxious to help the new fledgling nation combat any problems—whether domestic or foreign. He was thrilled to be part of a force commanded by Lieutenant General/President George Washington to squelch the Whisky Rebellion. Ironically the whisky makers in the west (some from Kentucky) were being taxed for their product, but still not being protected from marauding Indians. Fortunately the bulk of the hostile Indians were finally defeated by the Revolutionary war hero General "Mad" Anthony Wayne at the Battle of Fallen Timbers on August 20, 1794. This victory basically diminished most western people's notion that they were not being protected by the new American government. (Note 1)

Although Meriwether Lewis did not see any military action, he became an officer of the regular army under General Wayne. He was present when General Wayne signed the Treaty of Grenville on August 3, 1795—providing peace with Indians of the Ohio region. (Note 2)

With no Indians or battles to fight, Lewis soon found other enemies. His excessive drinking, his hot temper, and his Jeffersonian politics soon got Lewis in conflict with some of his fellow officers—who were mostly Federalists. Most of the differences were about the French Revolution—with Lewis and Jefferson in favor of the revolution.

On November 6, 1795 Lewis was brought before a general Courts Martial at General Wayne's headquarters. Lewis had caused a ruckus with a Lieutenant Elliot, and had challenged Elliot to a duel—both of which were against military regulations. Lewis pleaded "not guilty" to the charges and was acquitted after almost a week of testimony—perhaps because the old general influenced the decision. Anthony Wayne apparently did not like dissension in the ranks, and did not want the after effects if he punished a Virginia gentleman-soldier who had powerful friends in the new government. (Note 3)

General Wayne knew that he must keep the two combatants apart to avoid starting more trouble. He decided to transfer Meriwether Lewis to his newly created Chosen Rifle Company of Elite Riflemen-Sharpshooters. The captain of the company was also from Charlottesville, Virginia, had close family ties to Thomas Jefferson, and had distinguished himself in the Battle of Fallen Timbers. His name was William Clark! (Note 4)

Note 1, Stephen E. Ambrose, *Undaunted Courage,* (New York, NY, Simon and Schuster, 1996), Page 22.

Note 2, Ibid, Page 39. Note 3, Ibid, Page 45. Note 4, Ibid, Pages 45

CHAPTER 30

Clark & Lewis—Soldiers and Friends

By all indications all six of the Clark men were excellent marksmen with their Kentucky long rifles. Father John Clark had apparently taught his sons to shoot at a young age. In the 18th century in America it was necessary for the men in a family to protect the homestead, the women, and often hunt for food. If the hunt was not successful, they might not eat if the farm did not yield enough food.

The Clark family also supported the Revolutionary War effort by growing extra food for the troops, and sending five sons to fight honorably in the war. Jonathan served with George Washington at Valley Forge, and eventually became a general. John and Edmund became captains, and we of course know about George—also a general. Richard served with George after the Battle of Vincennes.

William was the youngest Clark son, having been born on August 1, 1770. He obviously had a number of expert brothers/marksmen to teach him how to shoot. Thus it would no surprise that William became captain of The Elite Riflemen-Sharpshooters under General "Mad" Anthony Wayne. After all, William had fought bravely at the Battle of Fallen Timbers, and had survived a number of other Indian skirmishes. In the fall of 1795, William had been in the army for four years. Although he was only twenty-five years old, his health was starting to fail—mainly due to poor army food during travel to his battles. He no doubt needed some of mother Ann Rogers Clark's home cooking. William was also beginning to worry more about his hero brother George's mounting financial problems. (Note 1)

When Meriwether Lewis was assigned to William's rifle company in November of 1795, one might assume it gave his spirits a lift to have a new person to talk with—particularly someone from his Charlottesville, Virginia area. Since there were no battles to fight, the two men had time to "hang out" together and discuss the problems of the world—and perhaps have a toddy or two.

This time for Meriwether Lewis, his drinking and political views found an ally. Clark's and Lewis' families were both Jeffersonians—eventually to become called Jeffersonian-Republicans. With General Wayne, Lewis had been at odds with a Lieutenant Elliot—who was a Federalist. Most career army officers were Federalists—mostly to protect their commissions and possible retirement benefits. The Federalists believed in a strong central government—much like the Democrats of today. The Jeffersonians believed in strong states rights, and only limited central powers—for the common good and protection from foreign invaders. Obviously Clark and Lewis had a lot to talk about, and probably agreed on most subjects. (Note 2)

Unfortunately for posterity not one word or letter exists about their six months together in the post Revolution American army. They obviously became great friends during this short period, but neither of them knew that this accidental happening would later have such a monumental effect on the history of America.

We would assume that Meriwether Lewis was disappointed when his new best friend left military service to return to Kentucky—to repair his health at Mulberry Hill in Louisville, and to help clear up some of George's tangled affairs.

Perhaps when William Clark left Meriwether Lewis in the spring of 1796—perhaps the first famous first Saturday in May—his parting words were: "Meriwether, this could be the beginning of a beautiful friendship".

Note 1, Stephen E. Ambrose, *Undaunted Courage,* (New York, NY, Simon and Schuster, 1996), Page 46.
Note 2, Ibid, Page 46.

CHAPTER 31

Meriwether Lewis—Life in the Army After William Clark

Meriwether Lewis stayed in the army for a total of four years. He was allowed to carry dispatches to various forts in the Ohio valley, which suited his roving nature. At first he got lost a number of times and barely survived once—by eating rotting bear meat—yuck! Lewis needed William Clark's knowledge of the Ohio valley.

In November of 1796 Lewis transferred to the First U. S. Infantry Regiment, perhaps because his new best friend was no longer with him in the more stationary rifle company. Lewis apparently became a favorite of General Wayne, and was allowed to take dispatches to and from the fort at Detroit. Ironically, that fort was now in American hands. Taking it had been the great unfulfilled ambition of George Rogers Clark.

Meriwether Lewis was also allowed a number of leaves from the army to visit his family in Virginia. He even had time to become active in the Masonic Order—the secret society that also had such famous members as George Washington, Benjamin Franklin, and Thomas Jefferson. Lewis reached a high level of Masonry in October of 1799—a Royal Arch Mason. William Clark would eventually become a Mason in 1809. (Note 1)

As Meriwether Lewis became more familiar with the Ohio Valley and the Ohio River, he was given more assignments to travel alone with dispatches. This also gave Lewis the opportunity to speculate in land. For example, in1797 he was able to buy 2,600 acres in northern

Kentucky for $.20 per acre ($520.00 total—but still a large sum for an army ensign to pay). In a letter to his mother in Virginia, Lewis told her that the Kentucky land was better than he had imagined it to be. (Note 2)

Lewis never got far enough down the Ohio River to connect with his friend William Clark. He did, however, write one letter to Clark, asking him about land availability in Ohio.

In March of 1799 Meriwether Lewis was promoted to lieutenant, and assigned to recruiting duties in Charlottesville, Virginia—his home town. When President John Adams opted not to add to the military, Lewis was reassigned to Detroit in 1800. It was a presidential election year—with Jefferson running against John Adams. At the Detroit assignment Lewis' hot temper flared again. He had heated political arguments with a Federalist officer and made his Jeffersonian-Republican points successfully made. Fortunately for Lewis no charges were made this time. (Note 3)

Meriwether Lewis was soon made regimental paymaster—a post created by Congress in 1799. This gave Lewis the opportunity to roam the Ohio Valley again and learn the politics of many of his fellow officers. He became well known for his honesty and punctuality. With his reputation growing, Meriwether Lewis was promoted to captain on December 5, 1800. That month the states also selected their delegates to the Electoral College—for the soon to be contested presidential election. (Note 4)

Note 1, Stephen E. Ambrose, *Undaunted Courage,* (New York, NY, Simon and Schuster, 1996), Page 47.

Note 2, Ibid, Page 47.

Note 3, Ibid, Page 49.

Note 4, Ibid, Page 50.

Chapter 32

Thomas Jefferson—The Third President—by a Nose

In modern day America there have been a number of hotly contested national elections. In 2004 the battle between Al Gore and George W. Bush was almost a dead heat—with Florida to be the swing state. The ballots were counted and recounted and "hanging chads" contested and examined over and over. It finally took the Supreme Court of Florida to rule that Bush had barely won.

In 2008 we had the famous contested recount for the U. S. Senate seat in Minnesota drag on for months—with the Democrat/comedian Al Franken barely winning.

We tend to think of this scenario as a new trend in elections. In fact the first real Presidential Election in America was the most hotly contested election in history. In the year of 1800 the delegates to pick the President were selected by the men who were the elected officials in each state. The common man (and of course no women) did not get to vote directly for his preferred candidate.

Thus when the delegates to the Electoral College voted in February of 1801, the votes were seventy-three each for Thomas Jefferson and his running mate, Aaron Burr of New York. President John Adams ran third with sixty-five votes. This dead heat created a political stalemate, with no one wanting to change their vote. The political arm twisting and possible bribery for delegates to change their votes sounds just like twenty-first century politics. (Note 1)

With the vote tied, the election was thrown into the House of Representatives where another stalemate ensued. The Federalists hated and feared Jefferson and tried to get at least one delegate to switch their vote to Burr. Finally Alexander Hamilton used his influence to break the tie. Although usually at odds with Jefferson, he felt that Jefferson was the lesser of two evils. On the thirty-sixth ballot, on February 17, 1801, Thomas Jefferson became the third President of The United States. (Note 2)

With more politics that sound very modern, John Adams started the precedent with his "midnight appointments'—filling the federal courts with Federalist judges, and appointing eighty-seven Federalist officers to the permanent military army. (Note 3)

Ironically the military appointments would lead to the ascension of Another of the Federalists' bitter enemies—the Jeffersonian-Republican Meriwether Lewis!

Note 1, Stephen E. Ambrose, *Undaunted Courage,* (New York, NY, Simon and Schuster, 1996), Page 50.

Note 2, Ibid, Page 50.

Note 3, Ibid, Page 50.

CHAPTER 33
Thomas Jefferson Hires an Ally

When Thomas Jefferson finally took the oath of office on March 4, 1801, he was faced with many Federalist enemies. John Adams had stacked the deck against Jefferson by his late appointments of Federalist judges and military officers.

Jefferson had apparently heard of Meriwether Lewis' clashes with Federalist leaning officers in the army, and Lewis preaching the Jeffersonian-Republican doctrine—favoring states rights. Thus, eleven days before his inauguration, Thomas Jefferson wrote to his Virginia neighborhood friend Meriwether Lewis to become his personal secretary and aide-de-camp. Jefferson was also interested in Lewis' knowledge of the western part of America, due to his interest in western expansion. (Note 1)

With the horse still the fastest method of transportation in 1801, it took two weeks for Jefferson's letter to reach Lewis, who was now serving at Fort Pitt. He was, of course, honored to be picked by his often defended hero—and now president—that Lewis sent an immediate reply. His letter of March 10, 1801 accepted the offer with profuse thanks. Lewis started for Washington at once, but spring rain, a lame horse, and bad roads caused him to take three weeks to arrive—barely sooner than when his letter arrived.

Thomas Jefferson had also written to Lewis' commander at Fort Pitt—General James Wilkinson—to give Meriwether Lewis a leave of absence from the army, but to retain his rank of captain and his eligibility for promotion. What a small world—this was the same guy who had trashed George Rogers Clark's career—making it more difficult for brother William to help settle George's tangled affairs. (Note 2)

As Meriwether Lewis settled into the President's House (it was not called The White House until it was rebuilt and painted white after having been burned during The War of 1812), he was thrilled to be working for his hero Thomas Jefferson. Lewis also enjoyed some perks, such as wining and dining with the movers and shakers of Washington, D. C.—such as they were in early America.

Lewis' quarters in the Presidents House were in what is now the east wing. In 1801 it was damp, cold, drafty, and depressing, with almost no furniture. Abigail Adams had hung her wash in that area, and had said that the twenty-three room unfinished mansion was way too big. (Note 3)

Nothing could dampen the spirits of the twenty-seven year old Meriwether Lewis, and he soon became busy routing out Federalist officers from the army—a high priority assignment from President Jefferson. Lewis actually had very few secretarial duties, since Jefferson wrote, and even copied his own speeches. Jefferson even sent his State of the Union speeches to Congress, feeling that delivering them in person was too much like a king pontificating to his subjects. Things have certainly changed in that regard. (Note 4)

Thomas Jefferson soon started to focus on his main agenda—the expansion of America to the west. He was afraid that England, France, or Spain would take over the continent west of the Mississippi River, and become a threat to our settlers in Kentucky, Tennessee, and the Northwest Territory. He did not want to lose that vast territory that had just been acquired—mostly due to the victories by his good friend—George Rogers Clark.

Here again the shrewd and brilliant Thomas Jefferson called upon his in-house expert of the known west—Meriwether Lewis.

Note 1, Stephen E. Ambrose, *Undaunted Courage,* (New York, NY, Simon and Schuster, 1996), Page 59.

Note 2, Ibid, Page 60.

Note 3, Ibid, Page 63.

Note 4, Ibid, Page 65.

CHAPTER 34
Thomas Jefferson—the Westward Worrier

As Thomas Jefferson settled into his office as America's third President in 1801, he soon turned his energies to his favorite project—westward expansion. With the Federalists somewhat diminished in power with Meriwether Lewis' help, Jefferson soon won the respect of Congress.

Jefferson had grown up with westward thinking people—his father having been part of The Loyal Land Company. This company had been ceded 800,000 acres west of the Appalachian Mountains in 1756. Due to the French and Indian War, however, they were never able to explore it. Even before he was President, but after the Revolution, Jefferson wrote George Rogers Clark about the possibility of leading a large force to explore the west. Clark wrote back, saying that a small force of three or four men might have more success—because the Indians would not think of them as invaders. Clark also declined the offer because of his mounting Revolutionary War financial problems. (Note 1)

Thomas Jefferson also had other reasons to focus on the west. He was worried that the aggressive French leader Napoleon Bonaparte might want to take Louisiana, and the Louisiana Territory from the more passive Spanish.

With Kentucky becoming a state in 1792, and Tennessee becoming the 15th state in 1794, more than one-third of America's exports and imports now came through New Orleans—by way of the Mississippi River. New Orleans and the Louisiana Territory had already changed hands a number of times when Thomas Jefferson became President in 1801. Early French explorers had claimed the territory for France. Not knowing or caring about this great asset they had, King Louis XV of

France gave the entire Louisiana Territory to Spain to repay a war debt France had incurred, while fighting as allies against England. (Note 2)

The Spanish did partially colonize their new territory by sending a few troops, and building forts at New Orleans and across the Mississippi River to the north at Saint Louis. As discussed in earlier chapters, Spain joined France and became America's ally against the British, helping George Rogers Clark to win the Revolutionary War in the west.

After the Revolution in 1784, the new Spanish governor of New Orleans decided to shut off the port of New Orleans for American shipping—unless tariffs were paid. Although the shipping ban was later rescinded, it gave our early American leaders—including Thomas Jefferson—the idea that America may soon need to control the Louisiana Territory in order to protect the rights of our growing westward population. In addition to the Spanish and French, Thomas Jefferson was also worried about the British trying to take back New Orleans—as well as the rest of America. (Note 3)

Jefferson's fears about France were confirmed in January of 1802, when he and the rest of America learned that Spain had ceded the Louisiana Territory back to France in a secret treaty of October 1, 1800. This, of course, happened before Jefferson became President in March of 1801. Thus it took sixteen months for the secret to come out. As Napoleon continued to conquer most of Europe, he had coerced Spain into giving back the Louisiana Territory—showing that he had ideas of expanding his empire to the American continent. (Note 4)

Thomas Jefferson—the brilliant author of The Declaration of Independence—now knew that he must act to deal with Napoleon if America was to remain a country. People in the fledgling republic did not want to be a colony again—the noble cause that many early Americans had fought and died for.

Note 1, Stephen E. Ambrose, *Undaunted Courage*, (New York, NY, Simon and Schuster, 1996), Page 68.

Note 2, Ibid, Page 72.

Note 3, Ibid, Page 72

Note 4, Charles A. Cerami, *Jefferson's Great Gamble*, (Naperville, IL, Sourcebooks, Inc., 2003), Page 41.

CHAPTER 35

Jefferson—The First Mississippi Gambler

In the early part of 1802, Thomas Jefferson and Congress now knew that America must deal with France for the right to keep trade open in Louisiana. We had to deal with the First Consul—Napoleon Bonaparte and his ministers. At this point in time, America was being represented by our Ambassador to Paris, Robert Livingston. Jefferson and his Secretary of State, James Madison did not like or trust Livingston—mostly because he was from New York. (Note 1)

At first Congress did not think that Jefferson was being aggressive enough about the Louisiana situation, and threatened to raise an army of 50,000 men to defend it. Soon, however, with the advice from the French family duPont, Jefferson and Congress were convinced that negotiating for Louisiana was the better and cheaper way to go. Although the du Ponts were not yet rich and famous, they were doing business in both France and America, and were savvy about politics in both places. (Note 2)

Jefferson and Madison soon ordered Livingston to start negotiations with Napoleon's shrewd minister Talleyrand. Despite his repeated requests, Livingston could not get Jefferson and Madison to give him a minimum or maximum figure to offer for the sale of Louisiana. (Note 3)

As the negotiations dragged on in 1802, Thomas Jefferson the impatient gambler, decided to send an exploration party into the Louisiana Territory—despite the fact that America did not own it. To this end in late summer or fall of 1802, Jefferson appointed his assistant Meriwether Lewis to command the expedition. In December of 1802 Jefferson convinced Congress to give him $2,500 for the mission. On the surface it was to be a way to extend America's trade possibilities up the Mississippi and Missouri Rivers. But in fact Jefferson wanted to have Lewis reach the Pacific Ocean. Jefferson had read accounts of the American sea captain Robert Gray, sailing his ship Columbia up a northwestern river from the Pacific Ocean in 1792, and Captain Cook's trip up and down the west coast in 1780. These events fixed the width of the North American continent at approximately 3,000 miles. (Note 4)

Although The United States was now in control of one-third of the continent, Thomas Jefferson in his brilliant mind had a vision of a United States of America "from sea to shining sea". He was convinced from his information of the day, that there was a northwest passage to the west coast—namely up the Missouri River, across a small portage, and down the Columbia River to the Pacific Ocean. The trade possibilities would be endless, and America might eventually claim the rest of the continent.

Knowing that such an undertaking would be difficult for one main commander, Jefferson ordered Meriwether Lewis to appoint a co-captain for the mission. In December of 1801, George Rogers Clark had written a letter to his old friend and now President, recommending his younger brother William Clark to some assignment for the government. Clark had said that William was of great character, and a jack-of-all-trades. When Meriwether Lewis decided to pick William Clark as his co-captain for the mission west, it is not known whether it was at Jefferson's request. It was mainly due to Lewis' friendship with William Clark in the army. In any case Jefferson approved Lewis' choice and agreed that Clark would be an equal commander—also with the rank of captain. Perhaps Jefferson in his infinite wisdom knew that Lewis was more the scientific type, and needed a partner with a proven military record. Who better would fit this requirement than William Clark of Kentucky. William, the former Captain of the Chosen Rifle Company, and also the younger brother of Revolutionary War General George Rogers Clark—the conqueror of the Northwest Territory. In any case and perhaps for more that one reason, on June 19, 1803, Meriwether Lewis sent a letter to William Clark of Louisville, Kentucky—offering him co-command of an expedition to explore parts unknown in the north American west. Thus, the letter became the most famous invitation in American history, and possibly the world. (Note 5)

The letter of invitation is amazing in that the two men had only been together for six months, and had not seen each other for eight years. In the letter Lewis outlines the mission to the west coast in very matter-of-fact language. Lewis concludes the letter as follows: "Thus my friend you have a summary view of the plan, the means and the objectives of this expedition. If therefore there is anything under those circumstances, in this enterprise, which would induce you to participate with me in it's fatiegues, it's dangers and it's honors, believe me there is no man on earth with whom I should feel equal pleasure in sharing them as with yourself". Lewis ends the famous invitation by offering William Clark a Captain's army commission—this with the approval of President Jefferson. (Note 6)

Note 1, Charles A. Cerami, *Jefferson's Great Gamble,* (Naperville, IL, Sourcebooks, Inc., 2003), Pages 77-78.

Note 2, Ibid, Page 139.

Note 3, Ibid, Pages 83-84.

Note 4, Stephen E. Ambrose, *Undaunted Courage* (New York, NY, Simon & Schuster, 1996), Page 76.

Note 5, Ibid, Page 97.

Note 6, Ibid, Pages 98-99.

CHAPTER 36
Finally—The Purchase of Louisiana

As the year of 1803 began, President Thomas Jefferson was very busy multi-tasking. He was teaching Meriwether Lewis how to use the sextant and other instruments—in order to determine a person's location in the wilderness. Jefferson was also teaching Lewis how to read maps—such as they were—and how to recognize flora and fauna on his trip to the west.

More importantly at this time Jefferson was trying to complete the negotiations with France for the purchase of Louisiana, and east and west Florida. To this end in early 1803 Jefferson sent his loyal Virginia friend James Monroe to Paris. Although Congress had only authorized only two million dollars for the sale, they had hinted at a much larger amount. Thus Jefferson gave Monroe a ball-park figure of nine million dollars. (Note 1)

Napoleon Bonaparte, The First Consul of France was totally in charge of France's destiny. Although France was theoretically being ruled by three Consuls, to replace the king system after the French Revolution, the other two Consuls are lost in obscurity. Napoleon was not even emperor yet, but already had the power of a dictator or a king.

Always the shrewd leader, Napoleon was planning to have his cake and eat it too (Marie Antoinette had not done well with her cake statement). Napoleon was quite willing to sell Louisiana to America—for a good price. Napoleon needed money to continue to support his large victorious army and navy, and he was about to declare war against England. After getting money from America for Louisiana, Napoleon planned to take it back by military force. To this end he had sent a large force of ships and troops to the island of Saint Domingue (present day Dominican Republic and Haiti) to prepare for the invasion. The trip from France to Saint Domingue is five thousand miles, but the island (which France had won from Spain) is only twelve hundred miles from New Orleans. Fortunately for America, native uprisings in Saint Domingue forced Napoleon to divert his forces to protect their territory. (Note 2)

When James Monroe arrived in Paris early in 1803, Napoleon realized that America was serious about buying Louisiana. To sweeten the pot—and hopefully get a higher price, Napoleon decided to include the entire Louisiana territory in the sale. This was easy for him to do, since no one knew how big it was, or how much area was included. Despite repeated attempts by Monroe and Livingston to Napoleon's main negotiator Talleyrand to define what was included in the Louisiana Territory, the sale area remained vague. Talleyrand did say, however, say that east and west Florida could not be included, since France had not received clear title of that area from Spain. (Note 3)

Perhaps Napoleon became more anxious to sell in early April of 1803 due to reading a London newspaper. The paper reported that the American Senate had voted to build fifteen gunboats to patrol the Mississippi River.

The weeks of haggling over price for the Louisiana Territory dragged on, with the price varying from eight million dollars to Napoleon's desire to get one hundred million francs (almost nineteen million dollars). Finally, Monroe the shrewd negotiator, got France to settle for fifteen million dollars total (eighty million francs). Even better for America—only sixty million francs would be paid to France in cash ($11,250,000), and the other twenty million francs ($3,750,000) would go to pay off American claims for France's seizure of American ships, crews, and cargos. (Note 4)

The final documents were signed in late April of 1803 and an official reception was held at The Louvre in Paris on May 1, with Monroe and Livingston wining and dining with Napoleon. The formal Louisiana Purchase treaty was signed and dated on May 2, 1803. Now would come the hard part in America. James Monroe, Robert Livingston, James Madison, and Thomas Jefferson would have to convince Congress to pay France seven times what they had authorized—for an unknown wilderness. (Note 5)

On May 13, 1803 Monroe and Livingston sent the signed treaty and their justification for their actions to President Jefferson—namely the fifteen million dollar price tag. This was done by sending the information with an American courier who left by a ship from LaHavre, France. There was no faster way.

By most accounts, the signed treaty arrived at the White House on July 3, 1803. Thus it took two months for the news of the Louisiana Purchase to reach America. Although some American newspapers casually reported the purchase, it was not until July 21 that President Thomas Jefferson officially proclaimed that the treaty had been signed. Now Jefferson—the Mississippi Gambler—had to sell Congress to approve the purchase. (Note 6)

As it is in present day America, Congress immediately started debating the expenditure of such a great sum of money—not billions or trillions, but a mere fifteen million—a large amount in 1803 for a young struggling country. President Jefferson's opposition party, the Federalists argued that we had since we bought New York for twenty-four dollars, it was ridiculous to pay fifteen million dollars for an unknown wilderness. (Note 7)

As the debates continued, Jefferson called for a session of Congress to meet on October 17, 1803, knowing that the treaty for Louisiana would be rescinded if not signed by October 30, 1803. In the end the purchase was approved by the Senate by a vote of twenty-four to seven. Since there were only fifteen states at the time, it is unclear how that there were thirty-one votes. It seems that John Quincy Adams—the son of President John Adams—had just been elected. Perhaps Massachusetts had three Senators for a short period of time. In any case John Quincy Adams crossed Federalist party lines to vote in favor of the world changing Louisiana Purchase. (Note 8)

Note 1, Charles A. Cerami, *Jefferson's Great Gamble* (Naperville, IL, Sourcebooks, Inc., 2003), Page 191.

Note 2, Ibid, Page 199.

Note 3, Ibid, Page 180.

Note 4, Ibid, Pages 203-204.

Note 5, Ibid, Page 205.

Note 6, Ibid, Page 208.

Note 7, Ibid, Page 210.

Note 8, Ibid, Page 214.

Chapter 37

Meanwhile—Back in Kentucky

Early in 1803 William Clark was living with his African-American slave York at the Clark family home in Louisville, Kentucky—Mulberry Hill. He had been there since leaving the army in 1796. He was, of course gone much of the time—riding thousands of miles to try and settle some of George's tangled business affairs. Otherwise William's life was fairly mundane. He had some knowledge of world affairs, and the possible purchase of Louisiana.

The parents of this great family had lived happily at Mulberry Hill until their deaths—Ann Rogers Clark on December 24, 1798, and John Clark in August of 1799. He had made a will that July splitting up his holdings among his sons and sons-in-laws. William was given Mulberry Hill and Jonathan was given land on which he built his plantation home—Trough Spring. It is on a sight selected by George, and built under the supervision of William in 1802. In 1803, George had moved to a log cabin on a hill in Indiana, overlooking the Ohio River. The Clark Parents had not been able to will anything to George—due to his situation with creditors. Ironically George Rogers Clark had gone west to find his own land due to the British law of primogeniture—which gave the oldest son (in this case Jonathan) the Virginia property. The law was no longer in effect after the Revolution, but poor George still got nothing. (Note 1)

In late July of 1803, word of the Louisiana Purchase reached Kentucky, setting off many celebrations. People from Ohio, Kentucky, Tennessee, and Louisiana now knew that they could trade up and down the Ohio and Mississippi Rivers without fear of tariffs or blockades.

We might assume that William, George, Jonathan, Lucy, and the rest of the Clarks got together for some parties, and perhaps partake of some Kentucky bourbon.

On July 29, 1803 a bigger shockwave may have reverberated through the Clark family, when William received the famous invitation from Meriwether Lewis. William, and possibly York moved in with George at his cabin—presumably to discuss the pros and cons of the invitation to explore the newly acquired territory.

Perhaps George said to William: "George Washington with some help from your brothers won the Revolution in the east—up to the Appalachian Mountains. I won freedom for Kentucky, Tennessee, and the Northwest Territory—up to the eastern shore of the Mississippi River. It is only fitting that you—my noble brother William should be one of the leaders to explore the rest of this great continent for The United States of America".

In any case, William and George must have quickly agreed to accept the offer, for William immediately sent the following reply: The enterprise &c. is Such as I have long anticipated and am much pleased with, and as my situation in life will admit of my absence the length of time necessary to accomplish such an undertaking I will cheerfully join you in an 'official Charrector' as mentioned in your letter,* and partake of the dangers, difficulties, and fatigues, and I anticipate the honors & rewards of the result of such an enterprise . . . . This is an undertaking fraited with many difeculties, but My friend I do assure you that no man lives with whome I would perfur to undertake Such a Trip &c. as yourself. (Note 2)

*Here Clark first wrote "on equal footing &c.", then crossed it out and substituted "as mentioned in your letter." (Note 2)

Once again Clark's reply to Lewis' letter shows the great friendship and mutual admiration and respect that had been forged between the two—soon to be great—men during their short time together in the army.

Equal command in any military situation normally does not work. What if two commanders disagree on an important matter? This co-command would become the rare exception to that problem.

Ironically William Clark was never officially promoted to Captain, and was only paid as a Lieutenant for the entire mission. Despite repeated attempts by Lewis to Secretary of War Dearborn to authorize the promotion, it never happened. Even Thomas Jefferson never got involved with the matter—perhaps due to other pressing matters, and his naivety about military matters. Clark was, however, still addressed by Lewis as Captain for the entire mission, and the men never learned of the problem. (Note 3)

Note 1, Kathleen Jennings, *Louisville's First Families: a Series of Genealogical Sketches,* Louisville, KY, The Standard Printing Co., 1920), Page 48.
Note 2, Stephen E. Ambrose, *Undaunted Courage,* (New York, NY, Simon & Schuster, 1996), Page 104.
Note 3, Ibid, Pages 99 & 135.

CHAPTER 38
Meriwether Lewis Heads to Kentucky

July 4, 1803 was a great day for Meriwether Lewis. On the previous day The White House had received word of the Louisiana Purchase. Although the deal would still need approval from Congress, Lewis could at least say with some confidence that he was exploring America's new territory.

Another reason for Lewis to celebrate was that he was ready to start his mission. He had arranged for guns and ammunition to be ready for him at the U. S. Army Arsenal in Harpers Ferry, Virginia. Ironically this would be the same armory that was taken over by abolitionist John Brown in October of 1859 in his effort to free African-American slaves—an act that had much to do with starting the Civil War in 1861.

On July 4, 1803, Lewis and America were, of course, celebrating the 27th anniversary of the signing of The Declaration of Independence—written by Lewis' boss and now President—Thomas Jefferson.

Even more important to Meriwether Lewis was the letter of credit signed by President Jefferson in its final version on July 4th, 1803. The letter allowed Lewis to draw credit from any agency of The U. S. Government—anywhere in America or around the world. It was probably the most unlimited letter of credit ever written in America. Other than the day that Lewis and Clark first saw the Pacific Ocean, July 4, 1803 was probably the best day in Meriwether Lewis' famous but short life. (Note 1)

On July 5, 1803, Lewis started for Harpers Ferry—the first step of many on the famous journey. Now he began to worry about the details of the mission. Would William Clark accept his offer to join the mission? Meriwether Lewis had made no backup plan or offer. Lewis was also worried that the large keelboat that he had contracted for would not be ready on schedule in Pittsburg. He was also concerned that the many supplies he had ordered in Philadelphia would get to Pittsburg on schedule. (Note 2)

Another thought may have worried Meriwether Lewis as he started out for Fredericktown (present Frederick, Maryland). Had he left before knowing about the official signing of the Louisiana Purchase, the mission would still be for possible trade routes up the Missouri River. Now that Lewis knew that he was to explore and claim America's new vast territory, he may have felt more pressure to succeed. He must find out what we bought—for Napoleon's minister Talleyrand never gave Monroe or Livingston a clear definition of the extent of the purchase.

Lewis now also had to convince the inhabitants of this vast territory that they were now citizens of The United States of America. This would turn out to be a difficult task, since almost all of the residents west of the Mississippi River were Indians—some peaceful, some warlike, and most tribes happy with the status quo. Lewis must now convince the Indians that they were now under the support and protection of the Great White Father in Washington—Thomas Jefferson.

Lewis also worried about sending any bad information about the mission, since the mainly Federalist Congress was not very happy about the large expenditure to which President Jefferson had committed America. Lewis, of course, wanted to send good reports to his boss.

Perhaps as Lewis reached Fredericktown on the evening of July 5th, he was refocused by learning that the ordered supplies were on their way to Pittsburg. On July 8th Lewis reached Harpers Ferry, and was happy with his tests of his new Kentucky long rifles and other armor. He then hired wagons to take the weapons to Pittsburg. (Note 3)

As Meriwether Lewis arrived in Pittsburg on July 15, 1803, his spirits fell again. The large keelboat—the main transportation for the mission—was way behind schedule. At least his supplies had arrived from Philadelphia, and the wagons of weapons arrived from Harpers Ferry on July 22nd.

Building the large keelboat dragged on—due to the boat builder's drinking habits and his lack of Lewis' urgency for completion of the project.

Great news came, however, on July 29th—William Clark's acceptance to be co-captain of the mission. Meriwether Lewis' fear of the unknown was probably diminished, now that he knew that his brave and capable friend would be there to share the trials and tribulations of the mission. (Note 4)

By August 5, 1803, only one side of the boat was planked, causing Lewis to be more frustrated. The boat builder's drunkenness and Lewis' complicated design of the keelboat added to the delay. The boat was fifty-five feet long, eight feet wide in the middle, and had a shallow draft. It had ten foot high decks fore and aft, with a cabin on the elevated aft deck. The hold of the boat was thirty-one feet long and could carry a cargo of about twelve tons. Across the deck were eleven benches—each to seat two rowers for the twenty-two oars. The boat also had a folding mast for sailing, and long poles for moving in shallow water. Since the Ohio River was very low that summer, Lewis bought a pirogue to carry some of the equipment, and thus lighten the load in the keelboat. A pirogue is basically a large flat bottomed canoe. Lewis also shipped some goods down river by wagon to Wheeling (now, of course, West Virginia), where he planned to buy another pirogue. (Note 5)

After more delays, causing Lewis to be in a constant state of frustration, the boat was finally ready on August 31, 1803. He had previously hired a few men to help sail the two craft down the Ohio. After loading the boats, Lewis was happy to be underway by 10:00 A. M.—starting the six hundred mile journey to meet his new partner William Clark in Louisville, Kentucky. (Note 6)

Note 1, Stephen E. Ambrose, *Undaunted Courage,* (New York, NY, Simon & Schuster, 1996), Page 101.
Note 2, Ibid, Page 103.
Note 3, Ibid, Page 103.
Note 4, Ibid, Page 104.
Note 5, Ibid, Pages 105-107.
Note 6, Ibid, Page 107.

CHAPTER 39

Lewis & Clark Meet in Indiana

While Meriwether Lewis was making his journey down the Ohio River in September of 1803, William Clark was busy in Louisville recruiting men for the trip west. The two Captains had agreed that the men must be young and hardy—preferably single and good hunters and marksmen. They, of course, had many applicants wanting to join the voyage, for adventure, fame and fortune.

On September 5, 1803 Meriwether Lewis reached Wheeling, where he purchased a second pirogue, and received the supplies sent by land from Pittsburg. By late September Lewis reached Cincinnati, Ohio and was only one hundred miles from his first main destination—Louisville, Kentucky. His trip had been fairly uneventful, except for getting stuck on some sandbars due to the shallowness of the river. Twice Lewis had to hire men and horses to pull the keelboat from a sandbar. Lewis also learned ways to shift the cargo and make the boat sail better. In short, the trip down the Ohio was a shakedown cruise for the long journey to come. (Note 1)

After resting his men for a week in Cincinnati, Lewis started the last part of the trip to Louisville in early October of 1803. On October 14, he arrived at the head of the Falls of the Ohio. (Note 2)

Once again the "Falls" were the beginning of a great historical journey. As chronicled previously in Chapter 10, George Rogers Clark had started his epic journey to conquer the Northwest Territory for America twenty-five years previously—in this exact same spot. Now Meriwether Lewis was about to join General Clark's younger brother William to start another monumental journey—to explore and claim the rest of the continent for America.

It may be remembered when George Rogers Clark (and his 175 troops) went down the falls in ten small boats, Simon Kenton the great Indian scout was in the lead boat. Kenton knew how to negotiate the small channel on the Indiana side of the river. In spite of a weird eclipse of the sun as they started, all of Clark's boats made it down the two and on half miles of limestone ledges.

This time the scenario was different for Meriwether Lewis and his boats. Although the two pirogues were similar in size to Clark's boats, the large fifty-five foot long keelboat would surely offer a different challenge.

Lewis was no doubt warned by William Clark about this obstacle, since on October 15, he hired pilots to take his boats through the rapids. It is not known if Simon Kenton was still in the area, or if the pilots had been taught by him. Perhaps when Lewis said in his educated eastern grammar: "may I hire you gentlemen to pilot my boats through the Falls ?", the crusty Kentucky boatmen said: "they aint falls, they is just over two miles of rocks". The pilots might also have said: "them two canoes will go thru O. K., but that big rascal may have its bottom banged up". (Note 3)

In any case the pilots got all three boats safely through the dangerous passage on the north bank of the Ohio River. Lewis tied up at Clarksville, and set off to meet his partner William Clark—who had been living with his older brother General George Rogers Clark. As Stephen Ambrose so aptly says it in his book *Undaunted Courage:* "When they shook hands, The Lewis and Clark Expedition Began". (Note 4)

This area is now part of the "Falls of the Ohio State Park", and there is a beautiful full size statue of Lewis and Clark shaking hands—overlooking what is left of the "Falls". William Clark is shown holding his hat, and Meriwether Lewis is holding his espontoon as they shake hands. The statue is engraved with Ambrose's famous quote.

Note 1, Stephen E. Ambrose, *Undaunted Courage,* (NewYork, NY, Simon & Schuster, 1996), Page 114
Note 2, Ibid, Page 117.
Note 3, Ibid, Page 117.

Photograph by Douglas C. Harrison

Chapter 40

The Corps of Discovery is Formed in Louisville, Kentucky

When Meriwether Lewis met William Clark in Clarksville in Indiana on October 15, 1803, they soon went to General George Rogers Clark's cabin overlooking the Ohio River. One can imagine the feast that George and William had prepared for Lewis and the few men he had brought with him.

No doubt there was much lively conversation among the three men late into that first night. One would assume that there were many adult beverages available—to celebrate the start of the epic mission. The old General/hero would have undoubtedly given the new heroes-to-be the benefit of his vast experiences farther west. He certainly shared his vast knowledge of the Indians he had dealt with.

We can only surmise what was said on that historic night above the Ohio, and across from Louisville—or how much useful advice was given to the young explorers by the old general. No one will ever know what was said, for no written word exists from that night of October 15, 1803. (Note 1)

In the days that followed, Lewis and Clark were busy enlisting men for the journey from the many applicants. Seven men were approved who had been previously picked by William Clark, and two who had been approved by Meriwether Lewis. When these nine men were sworn into the army by General George Rogers Clark, the Corps of Discovery was officially formed. (Note 2)

The "nine young men from Kentucky" performed nobly on the journey, and all but one made it back home to tell their stories. They were as follows: William Bratton, a hunter, blacksmith, and gunsmith; Joseph and Reuben Field who were good hunters, and knew salt making; Charles Floyd who was named a Sergeant by Clark, but who unfortunately became the only casualty on the trip; George Gibson, an expert hunter, marksman, fiddle player, and knew some Indian sign language; Nathaniel Pryor, who also became a sergeant, and later fought nobly in the battle of New Orleans; and George Shannon who was a good horseman, hunter, and singer. Meriwether Lewis picked two more men to make the total of nine as follows: John Coulter, a man of many talents, and John Shields, a skilled carpenter, gunsmith, blacksmith, and hunter. (Note 3)

William Clark, of course, made the tenth man from Kentucky for the Corps of Discovery. And then there was York, the African-American slave of Clark's—thus making the voyage a total of eleven young men from Kentucky.

York was apparently a tall able-bodied man who no choice but to go on the mission. By some accounts he had a wife, and possibly some children when he left Louisville in 1803. York was born in about 1772, a slave in Virginia—owned by the Clark family, his father York, Sr. having been father John Clark's personal slave. York was William Clark's boyhood companion and personal servant. When the Clark family moved to Kentucky, York of course went also. He would later become a valuable asset on the trip, but gained very little recognition or reward for his services. (Note 4)

On October 26, 1803, Lewis and Clark cast off their keelboat and a red and a white pirogue from Clarksville, Indiana—across the Ohio River from Louisville, Kentucky. Little could they have imagined that from that site you can now see a twenty-three thousand seat basketball arena—the new home of The University of Louisville Cardinals—whose colors are ironically—red and white. (Note 5)

Although the three boats were still undermanned, Lewis and Clark were promised more men down river at Fort Massac—an American outpost across the Ohio in Illinois (near present day Paducah, Kentucky).

Note 1, Stephen E. Ambrose, *Undaunted Courage,* (New York, NY, Simon & Schuster, 1996), Page 117.

Note 2, Ibid, Pages 117-118.

Note 3, Ibid, Page 118.

Note 4, Susan Griffin, *On the Threshold of Discovery,* (Louisville, KY, Publisher's Press, Inc., 2003), Page 9.

Note 5, Ibid, Page 9.

CHAPTER 41

George Drouillard—The Sign Talker

When the Corps of Discovery arrived at Fort Massac on November 11, 1803, they had been promised eight more men—needed for the mission. Upon arriving, Lewis and Clark found out that the men were not there yet.

At the recommendation of the fort's Commander, Lewis hired George Drouillard, a talented local woodsman to go to Tennessee and bring back the eight men to the Corps' winter camp north of St. Louis—a very tough assignment for any one person. (Note 1)

Perhaps it was divine intervention that George Drouillard would become one of the many valuable members of the historic mission. Drouillard, or "Drewer" as he was eventually called, since apparently no one could pronounce his name, was a half-breed. His father was French-Canadian, and his mother was a Shawnee Indian. How ironic is that, since the Shawnee had been George Roger's and William Clark's fiercest enemy in the past. George Drouillard was a multi-talented man. He was skilled in hunting, trapping, and scouting. More importantly, he knew a number of Indian languages, knew Indian ways, spoke English and French, and was a master of Indian sign language. (Note 2)

How lucky were Lewis and Clark to find a man like this to help communicate their message. They had theoretically planned every detail of the mission very carefully—with all the supplies and equipment needed to deal with the inhabitants up the Missouri River. Without proper communication with the Indians, the mission could have been a disaster. Fortunately for Lewis and Clark "Drewer", and later Charbonneau and Sacagawea would make their job much easier.

Note 1, Stephen E. Ambrose, *Undaunted Courage*, (New York, NY, Simon & Schuster, 1996), Page 118.
Note 2, Ibid, Pages 118-119.

CHAPTER 42

Slowly up the Mississippi to Saint Louis

On November 13, 1803 the Corps of Discovery left Fort Massac, and arrived at the mouth of the Ohio River a week later. It is there that the Ohio meets the mighty Mississippi. As they camped there William Clark again proved his value to the mission by measuring the width of the Ohio and Mississippi Rivers. He did this by using a measuring chain and surveying compass—a skill taught to William by big brother George.

Although the Ohio is formed in Pittsburg by the merging of the Allegheny and Monongahela Rivers, the Mississippi starts from a small stream out of the ground in northern Minnesota. When the river hits Minneapolis it is still only twenty to thirty feet wide. When Clark measured the Ohio, it was about thirty-six hundred feet wide, while the Mississippi had grown to over forty-two hundred feet wide. This made the two great rivers over a mile wide for Lewis and Clark to navigate the almost two hundred miles to Saint Louis—all upstream. (Note 1)

As the Corps of Discovery swung their keelboat and two pirogues away from the Ohio and started up the Mississippi, the Captains soon learned that the boats were badly undermanned. They would definitely need more men to be constantly going upstream against the unknown Missouri River. The Mississippi was perhaps fortunately a preview of things to come. After rowing and paddling for eight hours they had made only ten and one half miles. It took the boats four days to reach Cape Girardeau, Missouri, which is only twenty miles as the crow flies, but forty-eight miles by the winding Mississippi. The Captains obviously needed more men for the trip west. (Note 2)

On November 28, 1803, the Corps of Discovery arrived at Fort Kaskaskia on the Illinois side of the Mississippi, and only sixty miles south of Saint Louis. Here again the value of the Clarks of Kentucky can be seen. As it was chronicled in Chapter 11, Kaskaskia was the first major victory for George Rogers Clark in his conquest of the Northwest Territory for America from the British during the Revolutionary War. Now the fort would supply a dozen plus much needed men, and some gunpowder and supplies for the trip west. (Note 3)

On December 4, 1803, the captains split up. Clark would take the boats north to set up camp for the winter—directly across from the mouth of the Missouri River—in sight of their initial intended destination. Lewis would go by horseback—also on the Illinois side of the Mississippi to Cahokia—a settlement directly across from St. Louis. This, of course, was also won by George Rogers Clark during the Revolution. On December 8, Meriwether Lewis crossed the Mississippi River to meet with the Spanish Governor of St. Louis. This would set off a very interesting winter of 1803-1804 in the St. Louis area. At this time the Spanish officials did not officially know of the Louisiana Purchase by The United States of America.—compliments of Napoleon Bonaparte of France. (Note 4)

Note 1, Stephen E. Ambrose, *Undaunted Courage,* (New York, NY, Simon & Schuster, 1996), Page119.

Note 2, Ibid, Page 121.

Note 3, Ibid, Page 122.

Note 4, Ibid, Page 122.

CHAPTER 43

Winter Camp for Clark and St. Louis for Lewis—To Spring of 1804

When the Corps of Discovery arrived in St. Louis in early December of 1803, they had hoped to camp across the Mississippi at the mouth of the Missouri River—in order to get an early start up river in the spring. The Spanish governor of St. Louis told Lewis that they could not go into Spanish territory, since he had not received any official word of any land transfers.

Since the captains needed the support of the leaders in St. Louis, they did not argue the point. They did, however, find a four hundred acre sight twenty miles north of St. Louis on the Illinois side—across the Mississippi at the mouth of the Missouri River. On December 9 at Wood River the Corps of Discovery set up camp for the winter of 1803-1804. Captain William Clark would start to build huts for the men, modify the boats for the trip west, and start to train the men into a military force. (Note 1)

Meriwether Lewis had a much easier, but very necessary assignment. He would spend most of his time in St. Louis buying more supplies and recruiting more men for the trip west. When Lewis and Clark reached St. Louis, they had supplies for fifteen men, but knew that they needed at least forty men to man the keelboat and the two pirogues—since the trip up the Missouri was against the current.

Lewis immediately became popular with the merchants of St. Louis—he had President Thomas Jefferson's unlimited letter of credit—now days, a multi-million dollar platinum credit card. Lewis also got to stay in the best guest houses in St. Louis, and to be wined and dined by the city officials and prominent citizens—most likely due to their knowing that they would soon be governed by America. Perhaps this situation unfortunately led to Lewis' excessive drinking—before and after the success of the famous mission.

Meanwhile back at camp, Captain Clark was busy in his basically military role for the mission. He added lockers to the sides of the keelboat, with hinged lids—that could be raised to use as a shield from attacks. Clark also had Lewis purchase a bronze cannon which he mounted on a swivel at the front of the keelboat. The cannon could fire a one pound ball, or sixteen musket balls. He also added four blunderbusses—two to the stern of the keelboat, and one each to the pirogues. A blunderbuss is basically like a large shotgun. It was by orders of President Jefferson that the mission was to be peaceful. It is obvious that William Clark wanted the Corps of Discovery to be prepared for any warlike actions from Indians who did not see the American point-of-view. (Note 2)

Captain Clark must have had his spirits raised on December 16, when George Drouillard arrived at the winter camp with the eight soldiers promised from Tennessee. Although only four of the men would eventually be approved for the trip west, "Drewer" became an invaluable asset for the Corps of Discovery. (Note 3)

It appears that Clark and Drewer became friends that winter—despite the fact that William and brother George had fought against his relatives. Drewer finally agreed to go on the mission west—but not as a military private making fifteen dollars per month. Drewer would get twenty-five dollars per month, plus his money for the Tennessee trip, plus a salary advance which he sent to his Shawnee mother in Ohio. With Drewer's hunting, scouting, and interpreting skills, the extra money would be a good investment for the Corps of Discovery. (Note4)

As the winter of 1804 wore on in the mission camp, some men came and some men left, but by February, Captain Clark had approximately forty men trained and ready for the trip west. Meriwether Lewis apparently rewarded William Clark by bringing him to St. Louis for a few days—in late February of 1804. On February 20 Lewis also went back to St. Louis, leaving Sergeant Ordway in charge of the camp. At this point there were desertions and discipline problems—showing that only the Co-captains firm hands had the total respect of the enlisted men. Also, the men were getting anxious to go up the Missouri River to start their adventure—rather than the boring life of winter camp. (Note 5)

Meanwhile in early March of 1804, the transition of St. Louis finally happened. The Louisiana Purchase to America became official. As a repeat of the ceremonies that took place in New Orleans, on December of 1803, the officials of St. Louis did their part. On March 9, Spain ceded St. Louis and its western territories to France. As the French flag replaced the Spanish one, a great cheer went up from the mostly French population of St. Louis. After one day—on March 10, 1804—the French tri-color came down, and the stars and stripes rose over St. Louis for the first time. (Note 6)

The Lewis and Clark mission to explore the western part of the Louisiana Purchase was now almost ready. Spring would soon be here, and the Corps of Discovery could now cross the Mississippi into American territory up the Missouri—not Spanish or French, but actually Native-American—many of whom were happy with their lifestyle.

Note 1, Stephen E. Ambrose, *Undaunted Courage,* (New York, NY, Simon & Schuster, 1996), Pages 123-124.

Note 2, Ibid, Pages 127-128.

Note 3, Ibid, Page126.

Note 4, Ibid, Page 119.

Note 5, Ibid, Pages 128-129.

Note 6, Ibid, Pages 129-130.

Chapter 44
Final Preparations for the Mission West

As March turned into April, and April turned into May of 1804, Meriwether Lewis continued to buy more supplies in St. Louis on his "platinum credit card"—backed by President Jefferson. No doubt the supplies were needed, but Lewis apparently enjoyed the many perks he received from the St. Louis merchants.

The Captains knew how to work hard and play hard. For example, on Friday April 7, Lewis and Clark crossed the Mississippi by canoe from Camp Wood to St. Louis. They were greeted by a Captain Stoddard and made guests in his home. A dinner and ball was then held at Stoddard's home—in honor of the Corps of Discovery. Fifty of St. Louis' prominent citizens and their wives were invited, and the party lasted until 9:00 A. M. Sunday. Predictably, Clark wrote in his journal Sunday night: "No business today". (Note 1)

Meanwhile back at Wood River, the troops were getting very restless about starting the mission. They had very few perks to break the monotony of camp life. Finally, on May 8, 1804, some action took place. Captain Clark took the loaded keelboat and the two pirogues on a dry run in the Mississippi River. They now had twenty-two private soldiers and three sergeants in the keelboat. They also had six soldiers and a corporal in one pirogue, and eight French voyagers in the other pirogue. The Frenchmen were there to introduce the men from the Corps of Discovery to the Mandan Indians up the Missouri River. The Frenchmen would then return to St. Louis in the large keelboat. Some misconceptions of the mission exist—including a Hollywood movie that has the troops and the captains hauling the keelboat up a portage to another navigable river. This, of course, never happened.

After shifting some cargo from the stern to the bow of the keelboat, Captain Clark declared that all was ready to start the mission. Clark correctly decided that it would be better to hit a submerged log, or an uprooted tree, head-on with the strongly made bow of the keelboat. Perhaps the Captain of the Titanic should have learned a lesson from William Clark of Kentucky. In any case, the Corps of Discovery was ready to go up the mostly unexplored Missouri River. (Note 2)

Note 1, Stephen E. Ambrose, *Undaunted Courage,* (New York, NY, Simon & Schuster, 1996), Page 133.
Note 2, Ibid, Page 136.

CHAPTER 45

Captain William Clark Initiates the Mission West

On May 14, 1803 the Corps of Discovery finally left their camp at Wood River—with Captain Clark in Charge. Meriwether Lewis was still in St. Louis settling accounts and giving his final farewells to the local people who had befriended—and made a healthy profit from—the Corps of Discovery. (Note 1)

Since the boats left late in the day, and had to cross the Mississippi River from the camp, they only made four miles up the Missouri the first day. As the boats continued up river, they reached the last official white settlement on the Missouri River—St. Charles—about thirty miles up river. On May 20th, Lewis finally caught up with the boats at St. Charles, by riding a horse from St. Louis—accompanied by over a dozen local well-wishers.

The boats then left St. Charles late the next day and only make three miles up the Missouri before dark. Thus, one might say that the first full day of the mission west happened on May 22, 1804 when the boats left at 6:00 A. M. that day. (Note 2)

The Captains soon found out that the trip was going to be no piece-of-cake. The Missouri was muddy and flooded in the spring of 1804, and there were many large logs and uprooted trees to be dodged by the heavily loaded keelboat and the two pirogues.

Note 1, Stephen E. Ambrose, *Undaunted Courage*, (New York, NY, Simon & Schuster, 1996), Page 137.

Note 2, Ibid, Pages 138-139.

CHAPTER 46

Lewis and Clark Meet another Kentucky Pioneer—Daniel Boone?????

After thinking that the Captains had seen the last white people until their return to St. Charles or St. Louis, they unexpectedly came upon a small farming community of white people from Kentucky. This happened on May 25, 1804—only eleven days from their departure.

Here again is one of history's mysteries. The settlement had been created by in 1799 on a land grant by the Spanish Government to Daniel Boone. He apparently had done this because of his failed claims of land in Kentucky. (Note 1)

Although Daniel Boone moved there permanently in 1805, we do not know if he met with Lewis and Clark on that day. Surely William Clark would have written a few words in his journal about this occasion. How sad is this—Clark only recorded that day: "The people at this village is pore, houses small, they sent us milk & eggs to eat". (Note 2)

Now the Corps of Discovery was really off into the unknown—where no white American had ever ventured. As they slowly made their way up the winding Missouri in June and July of 1804, the trip was fairly uneventful. Except for problems with sandbars and floating logs to dodge, the boats were making fairly good progress—by rowing, poling, or by sailing.

By the end of July 1804, the expedition had gone 640 miles up the Missouri River—without seeing any Indians. All of the Indians who lived near the river were out on the prairie hunting buffalo. (Note 3)

Note 1. http://en.wikipedia.org/wiki/Daniel_Boone, Page 8.

Note 2. Stephen Ambrose, *Undaunted Courage,* (New York, Simon and Schuster, 1996), Page 144.

Note 3. Ibid, Page 151.

Chapter 47

Finally, Some Indians to Tell and Sell the Story Of Their New American Father

On August 1, 1804, the Corps of Discovery celebrated Captain William Clarks thirty-fourth birthday. The next day a party of about two-hundred fifty Otos, and a few Missouri Indians arrived in camp. They were mainly farming and hunting tribes, that had been decimated by smallpox. (Note 1)

On August 3, the Corps of Discovery held their first council with the Indians, and called it Council Bluff. (Present day Council Bluffs, Iowa). The Captains held their first "dog and pony show", with the troops marching in formation, and firing their Kentucky long rifles. Captain Lewis made his first speech through a French interpreter who had accompanied the Otos. He told them about their new "Great White Father" in Washington—who would now protect and provide for them. The Captains then handed out trinkets and Jefferson Peace Medals. (Note 2)

The Oto chiefs were fairly receptive to the new scenario, but requested gun powder and whiskey. Since Lewis wanted some of the chiefs to go to Washington—per Jefferson's orders—he gave them a canister of powder, fifty balls and a bottle of whiskey. The main chief, called Little Thief, agreed to go to Washington the following spring. Although Little Thief never made it to D. C., we now have big thieves there—they are called Congressmen, Senators, and sometimes lately—the President. Thus the first meeting with Native Americans by the Corps of Discovery went fairly well. This would not always be the case, however, with the warlike Sioux soon to be encountered. (Note 3)

Note 1, Stephen E. Ambrose, *Undaunted Courage,* (New York, NY, Simon & Schuster, 1996), Pages 155.

Note 2, Ibid, Page 156.

Note 3, Ibid, Page 158.

CHAPTER 48
The First—and Last Casualty of the Mission

Soon the troops left the peaceful Otos, and headed up the Missouri River. Unfortunately on August 20, 1804 Sergeant Floyd died. He had been ill for some time, and apparently succumbed to a ruptured appendix. Miraculously, with all the perils of this 10,000 mile trip, this was the only fatality. Sergeant Floyd was buried with full military honors on a bluff overlooking the Missouri River. Thus, he became the first American soldier to be buried west of the Mississippi River. (Note 1)

Since the sergeant was one of the "nine men of Kentucky", and appointed by Captain Clark, Clark performed the eulogy—that he had written. It went as follows: "This man at all times gave us proofs of his firmness and determined resolution to doe service to his Countery and honor to himself". (Note 2)

Two days later and forty-one miles up the Missouri, the captains decided to let the privates elect Sargeant Floyd's replacement—again showing their flexibility in various situations. A Private Gass won by a large margin, thus making this the first election ever held west of the Mississippi River. (Note 3)

Note 1, Stephen E. Ambrose, *Undaunted Courage,* (New York, NY, Simon & Schuster, 1996), Page 160.

Note 2, Ibid, Pages 160-161.

Note 3, Ibid, Page 161.

CHAPTER 49
Close Encounters of the Sioux Kind

On August 27, 1804 the Corps of Discovery encountered the Yankton Sioux Indians—the last friendly Indians they would see for a while. The reason was that the Yankton Sioux did business in St. Louis through French traders. The warlike Teton Sioux and the Arikaras to the north traded only with the British—to the north in Canada.

When a few young Yankton braves approached the expedition's camp, and appeared to be friendly, the Captains ordered Sergeant Prior to go to their camp and invite some Yankton chiefs for a council. The sergeant was treated well, and returned with some chiefs and a description of their camp. He said that their dwellings were very colorful and conical in shape. There were approximately forty in number, with a dozen or more Indians per tent. Thus, Sergeant Pryor became the first white American to describe an Indian teepee. (Note 1)

The Captains soon gave the standard American message, with help from an old French interpreter Mr. Dorian—whom the Oto Indians had brought with them. The Captains gave out trinkets, tobacco, and medals. Although the Yankton Sioux chiefs were disappointed with the gifts—they wanted powder—they remained friendly. They did, however, warn the Captains that the Teton Sioux—their former brothers—would not be friendly, and might try to stop the Corps of Discovery at their camp near the Missouri River. (Note 2)

The expedition continued upstream peacefully until September 23, 1804, when they were confronted by some young Teton Sioux braves. Using sign language, Drouillard found out that there were two bands of Teton Sioux nearby—one with sixty lodges, and one with eighty lodges. With approximately ten Indians per lodge, it meant that there were about fourteen hundred Teton Sioux in the area. Thus, the Corps of Discovery was outnumbered about twenty-eight to one. (Note 3)

It was here that Lewis and Clark were to be gravely tested. They first met with three chiefs and many warriors, and gave an abbreviated "dog and pony show". It did not go over well, partly due to their lack of a good interpreter. The Teton Sioux chiefs were not happy with their "worthless medals and silly Hats". They apparently wanted whiskey, guns, powder, and balls. The Captains did invite the chiefs aboard the keelboat for whiskey and an overnight stay. Lewis and Clark and most of the soldiers even went to the camp of the main Teton chief—Black Buffalo. The entire mission could have been wiped out right there—except for the brave front the Captains and the crew presented. The Teton Sioux were the terrorists of their day—in that part of the Missouri River. Fortunately for the Corps of Discovery, these Indians did not want to lose large numbers of warriors in battle. They preferred to attack unarmed parties by surprise. (Note 4)

When the Teton chiefs were allowed to spend another night on the keelboat, they did not want to leave. It was not like a luxury cruise ship of modern times but may have seemed like it to the chiefs—compared to their primitive lodges. The chiefs demanded a canoe full of presents. Finally Captain Clark had had enough. He forced the chiefs ashore, and prepared the keelboat for action. All of the soldiers manned their rifles, Clark drew his sword, and held a lighted a lighted match over the swivel gun on the bow of the keelboat. The Indians backed down, but would not release the rope holding the keelboat on the shore. After more threats from both sides, Captain Clark persuaded the main Teton Sioux chief, Black Buffalo to have his braves release the rope—by throwing him a carrot of tobacco (a plug of tobacco rolled up into a shape similar to a carrot). (Note 5)

After four very tense days the boats headed up the Missouri again. With a south wind, the Captains hoisted the sail and they made twenty miles that day. They stayed on a sandbar in the middle of the Missouri—just in case they had been followed. The men were refreshed with whiskey. Who wouldn't need a drink after all of those stressful events. Captain Clark finally got to sleep—after being up for four straight days and nights.

This confrontation became the closest thing to a major battle with Native Americans on the entire expedition. The bravery and courage of Lewis and Clark and their men prevented what could have been a massacre—and the end of the mission. (Note 6)

Note 1, Stephen E. Ambrose, *Undaunted Courage,* (New York, NY, Simon & Schuster, 1996), Pages 161-162.

Note 2, Ibid, Page 164.

Note 3, Ibid, Page 168.

Note 4, Ibid, Page169.

Note 5, Ibid, Page 170-175.

Note 6, Ibid, Page 175.

CHAPTER 50

More Indians on the Missouri River—The Arikaras, The Mandans, and The Hidatsas

The Corps of Discovery continued uneventfully up the Missouri River into the fall of 1804. The scenery was beautiful, and the Captains enjoyed a more relaxing cruise for a change. They were in what is present day northern South Dakota. While Captain Clark directed the boats, Captain Lewis would explore the land nearby—only joining the rest of the mission at night. He could walk as much as thirty miles a day with his long stride—armed only with his rifle, his espontoon, and his faithful dog Seaman. An espontoon is a sort of pike, six feet tall with a wooden shaft and a metal blade. It also had a small cross at shoulder height to be used as a support for his long rifle. Lewis did carry a field journal in order to record new plants, animals, minerals, and the lay of the land. Meriwether Lewis was possibly happiest in this type of carefree environment. (Note 1)

On October 6, 1804, the voyagers reached the Arikara Indian villages, which were situated on a three mile long island in the Missouri. The Captains were still very much on guard, since the Arikaras were allies of the Teton Sioux. As it turned out, they were basically farmers for the Sioux and very peaceful. They had been decimated by smallpox from thirty thousand down to their current population of two thousand. (Note 2)

This time the Captains were fortunate to find a good interpreter, who had been living with the Arikara Indians. Their "dog and pony show" went fairly well, and many of the braves became very friendly with the men of the expedition. The braves offered their squaws for sex with the white men—believing that the act would transfer power to themselves. York was in demand—due to the color of his skin. The Captains did not participate, but allowed the men to take part—not wanting to offend the Indians. (Note 3)

On October 14, 1904, the Corps of Discovery started up the Missouri again. The days were getting shorter and the nights colder, making it necessary to soon find a place to build a winter camp. They had learned that the Mandan Villages were a great trading center, and thus fairly peaceful.

On October 24th the Captains met their first Mandans—Chief Big White and a hunting party of twenty-five braves. (Big White would eventually go to Washington). (Note 4)

The Mandans consisted of two villages and their allies the Hidatsas had three villages nearby. Although both tribes seemed very friendly toward the expedition, the Captains were still leery of Indian tricks—due mostly to their confrontation with the Teton Sioux. Thus, Lewis and Clark agreed that only one of them would leave the keelboat at the same time. What a great "dynamic duo" they turned out to be. After a number of days and meeting with the various chiefs, the Captains decided to stay nearby for the winter, but in their own fort. On November 3, 1804, the Corps of Discovery started to build Fort Mandan—their refuge from what would turn out to be a very cold North Dakota winter. (Note 5)

Note 1, Stephen E. Ambrose, *Undaunted Courage,* (New York, NY, Simon & Schuster, 1996), Page 177.

Note 2, Ibid, Page 178.

Note 3, Ibid, Page 180.

Note 4, Ibid, Page 183.

Note 5, Ibid, Page 184-186.

CHAPTER 51

The Captains Find a Treasure—Named Sacagawea

One day after the Corps of Discovery started Fort Mandan, Lewis and Clark were approached by a French-Canadian named Toussaint Charbonneau. He informed the Captains that he had two squaws that were Shoshone (or Snake) Indians. His "wives" were teen-agers who had been captured four years earlier by a Hidatsa raiding party. Charbonneau had won the girls on a bet with the Hidatsa—perhaps in a poker game. The captains gladly accepted his offer, now more aware of the importance of good communication. Their lack of a good interpreter had almost caused a major disaster with the Teton Sioux. (Note 1)

The interpretation would go as follows: the "wives" would talk to Charbonneau in Hidatsa; then he would talk to Drouillard in French, who would then talk to the Captains in English. Although this was a cumbersome process, it was far better than nothing. Sacagawea was selected to go with the Corps of Discovery, even though she was only about fifteen years old, and six months pregnant—perhaps because of her better command of the various languages, or that Charbonneau knew that her brother was a Shoshone chief. (Note 2)

The Captains also wanted Sacagawea since her tribe lived in the Rocky Mountains—near the mouth of the Missouri River. The Shoshones were also known to have horses—something the Captains would need for what they thought would be a short trip. They would go from the end of the Missouri, cross the Rocky Mountains, and soon get to the Columbia River.

Work continued on Fort Mandan. When it was finished it consisted of eighteen foot high walls, a palisade on the river side, a gate, a sentry post, and the ever present swivel gun—removed from the keelboat. There were two rows of huts inside the fort, one of which was given to the captains' new interpreters—Charbonneau and Sacagawea. Now the Corps of Discovery was ready for the very cold winter of 1804-1805 to come.

Note 1, Stephen E. Ambrose, *Undaunted Courage,* (New York, NY, Simon & Schuster, 1996), Page 187.

Note 2, Ibid, Page 187.

Note 3, Ibid, Pages 186-187.

CHAPTER 52

The Extremely Cold Winter with the Mandans of 1804-1805

On December 7, 1804, Captain Lewis went hunting with the Mandans. It was forty-five degrees below zero, making it the coldest day of the year—with winter still thirteen days away. The keelboat was already frozen in the Missouri River. (Note 1)

The Corps of Discovery did maintain good relations with the Mandan Indians. There were many parties over Christmas, and New Years. They spent time talking, trading, joking, and having sexual relations. Here again York became popular—just as he had been with the Arikaras. The Mandans had never seen a black person, and considered York to be a god. At first the Mandan chiefs would rub his skin, trying to wipe the color off. Since he was considered to be of holy status, the Mandans ordered their squaws to have sex with York. Their belief was that this act would transfer back to them, and allow them to be more holy. Obviously, with the large number of nasty divorces in the world for infidelity, this practice is not popular today's society. Lewis and Clark apparently ordered York to comply with the Mandan's requests—not wanting to make the Indians mad. How ironic is it, that the Captains later allowed York to vote the next winter on their west coast location—along with Sacagawea. (Note 2)

On February 5, 1805, Sacagawea went into a difficult labor. She was only fifteen at the time. Meriwether Lewis was the closest thing the Corps of Discovery had to a doctor. He mixed some parts of a rattle from a rattlesnake with water, and gave the mixture to Sacagawea. It seemed to work, and she delivered a healthy baby boy ten minutes later. Here was another irony—she was a Shoshone/Snake Indian. Sacagawea named her son Jean Baptiste Charbonneau. (Note 3)

The rest of the winter of 1805 passed slowly but quietly, with the men just trying to stay warm, and repairing their equipment for the western trip to come. Perhaps some of the men started to miss their homes, with the cries and sounds of a baby nearby—possibly reminding them of a little brother or sister.

The Captains were now worried that a teenager with a baby on her back could not make the trip. They would soon find out how tough and valuable she would become. Charbonneau on the other hand, would turn out to be of little value to the mission—except for some interpreting help. He even tried to dictate terms for his and Sacagawea's employment—but gave in as the Captains stood firm on their terms. He was to share work duties with the rest of the troops. (Note 4)

Note 1, Stephen E. Ambrose, *Undaunted Courage,* (New York, NY, Simon & Schuster, 1996), Page 190.

Note 2, Ibid, Pages 193-195.

Note 3, Ibid, Page 197.

Note 4, Ibid, Page 198.

CHAPTER 53

Up the Missouri Again— But Lighter and Faster

Finally spring started to come along the Missouri at Fort Mandan in March of 1805. The permanent party to go west was now complete. It consisted of three squads of soldiers—each having a sergeant, the two Captains and five other people. They were as follows: Drouillard, York, Charbonneau, Sacagawea, and her baby boy Jean Baptiste (or Pomp—a name Captain Clark had given him). The troops were kept busy getting their equipment ready, and building six new canoes for the trip west. The Captains plan was to send the keelboat back to St. Louis with the French voyagers. The Corps of Discovery would continue up the Missouri River in the two pirogues and the six new canoes. The large keelboat had served the expedition well—particularly against hostile Indians—but would soon be useless as the Missouri became shallower and narrower. (Note 1)

The keelboat was loaded with written reports from the Captains, 108 botanical specimens, sixty-eight mineral specimens, and various animal skins. A masterpiece of a map was also sent that was made by William Clark. The map was the first accurate document from St. Louis to Fort Mandan, and included all rivers feeding into the Missouri. (Note 2)

On April 7, 1805, the expedition split—with the loaded keelboat heading south, and the heavily loaded pirogues and canoes heading northwest. Lewis sent a corporal, some privates, and the four Frenchmen from St. Louis on the keelboat. The men were warned by the Captains to be wary of hostile Indians on the return trip—particularly the Teton Sioux. The keelboat did now, however, have the advantage of—going with the flow—as the saying goes. The Corps of Discovery could also now make better time by rowing their lighter boats upstream—once again going where no white American had ever been. (Note 3)

Note 1, Stephen E. Ambrose, *Undaunted Courage,* (New York, NY, Simon & Schuster, 1996), Page 210.

Note 2, Ibid, Pages 206-207.

Note 3, Ibid, Page 210.

CHAPTER 54

A Quandary at a Fork in the Missouri

The Corps of Discovery was now making good time up the Missouri—going ninety-three miles in the first four days. The white pirogue became the flagship for the mission. It contained the two Captains, Drouillard, Charbonneau, Sacagawea, Pomp, and six paddlers. It also contained the journals, the medical supplies, a field desk, trinkets for the Indians, gunpowder, and a teepee for use at night. The red pirogue contained more supplies and six paddlers. The six canoes were paddled by three paddlers each. The teepee was used to house those from the flagship, while the other men slept on the ground. (Note 1)

The trip went well until April 13, when a gust of wind almost overturned the white pirogue. It was under sail, with Charbonneau at the tiller. For some reason both Captains were on shore—which violated their own policy. As Charbonneau panicked, he turned the boat sideways, instead of heading directly into the wind. This caused the pirogue to fill with water. As the paddlers frantically bailed, Sacagawea remained calm as she grabbed all of the floating important papers from being washed away—and with a baby on her back. This event started to prove her great value to the mission—and Charbonneau's lack of any value. Sacagawea would soon also help the men's diet by searching for berries, fruit, and edible roots—all of which were badly needed to add some variety to their meat only meals. (Note 2)

On June 9, 1805, the Corps of Discovery reached a fork in the Missouri River. No one in the party—including Sacagawea, who had never been there before—knew which fork was the Missouri (the north fork would turn out to be the Marias River). The Captains decided to split up, with Captain Clark taking the boats up the north fork, and Captain Lewis taking a small party by land up the west fork. Before anyone left, it was decided to hide the red pirogue, and bury a cache of supplies—to be used on the return trip. (Note 3)

The Captains plan was simple but clever as usual. They had been told by the Hidatsa Indians that there were falls on the Missouri River, and then perhaps a short trip over the Rocky Mountains to the Columbia River. Since both branches of the fork faced the Rocky Mountains, he who found the mountains first was on the wrong river. He who found the falls of the Missouri first would send a runner to have the two missions rejoined—at the base of the falls. (Note 4)

Note 1, Stephen E. Ambrose, *Undaunted Courage,* (New York, NY, Simon & Schuster, 1996), Pages 213.
Note 2, Ibid, Pages 224-225.
Note 3, Ibid, Pages 233-234.
Note 4, Ibid, Pages 234-235.

CHAPTER 55

Lewis Discovers the Falls— Good News and Bad News

On June 13, 1805, after a four day hike of fifty miles up the Missouri River, Captain Lewis began to hear a loud noise. Upon going further, he saw what looked like a cloud of smoke. It was, of course, a misty vapor rising from the falls of the Missouri. Meriwether Lewis had become the first American to see the falls of the Missouri River. He immediately sent a runner to find Captain Clark in order to share his jubilation. It was beginning to appear that Lewis' boss, President Jefferson was right about the existence of a Northwest Passage. (Note 1)

On June 16, 1805, the Corps of Discovery was reunited below the falls that Captain Lewis had discovered. The first bad news was that Sacagawea was gravely ill—partly to being bled—the proper but incorrect procedure that doctors prescribed at the time. Fortunately "Doctor" Lewis came again to her rescue—with sulfur water and a poultice. The Captains were, of course, worried about Sacagawea's health. This was mostly due to the fact that her Shoshone tribe lived nearby up the Missouri—and her ability to translate their message. (Note 2)

Captain Clark was put in charge of the portage, while Captain Lewis went up river to continue to explore the unknown Missouri River. More bad news—Captain Lewis soon returned, reporting that he had encountered four more falls, making the total of five falls a twelve mile portage. He had also seen some mountains in the distance. Perhaps some depression was starting to enter the great mind of Meriwether

Lewis. He now knew that he must report to his boss, President Jefferson that the Northwest Passage was not going to be as easy as originally thought. (Note 3)

Shortly after Captain Clark set off to explore the route of the portage, Captain Lewis discovered a large cottonwood tree—twenty-two inches in diameter. Lewis put six men to work sawing the tree crosswise to make wheels. He then had the hardwood mast of the white pirogue cut to make axles. The balance of the tree would be made into tongues and bodies to make two wagons—to haul supplies up the portage. Here again, the ingenuity of both captains is shown—in order to live off of the land as necessary. (Note 4)

Note 1, Stephen E. Ambrose, *Undaunted Courage,* (New York, NY, Simon & Schuster, 1996), Pages 236-237. ote 2, Ibid Pages 241-242.

Note 3, Ibid, Page 242.

Note 4, Ibid, Page 242.

CHAPTER 56
Sacagawea to the Rescue—Again and Again

The portage over the twelve miles of five falls of the Missouri River took the Corps of Discovery almost an entire month. Fortunately Captain Clark had sent hunters to find cottonwood trees above the falls—which could be made into canoes. These would be needed to be used in lieu of the pirogues and an iron framed boat that Meriwether Lewis had brought—having had it made in Harpers Ferry, Virginia. Although covered with skins, the boat could not be kept from leaking. Thus, the cottonwood trees were felled and hollowed out for canoes. (Note 1)

As the Corps of Discovery continued up the Missouri, the river was getting shallower, and the mountains were looming larger. As the trip became more difficult, the morale of the men was getting lower. On July 22, 1805, Sacagawea recognized this part of the river—where she had been as a young girl. This gave a great boost to the spirits of all the men. She also told the Captains that the three forks of the Missouri were not far ahead. (Note 2)

After five more difficult days of rowing and poling against an increasingly swifter and shallower Missouri, the Corps of Discovery was elated to arrive at the three forks. The Captains decided to name the three rivers. The left fork that came in from the southeast was named for the Secretary of the Treasury—Albert Gallatin. The middle fork was named for James Madison, the Secretary of State. The southwest fork was named for the Captains mentor—President Thomas Jefferson. The three rivers still go by the same names—with the Gallatin and the Madison flowing from nearby Yellowstone Park in Wyoming, and meeting in the small town of Three Forks, Montana. The Jefferson—which the Captains decided to take west, was and is the final leg of the Missouri River. (Note 3)

After resting for two days at three forks, the Corps of Discovery started up the Jefferson/Missouri River. On August 7, 1805, they made seven miles west. The next day they made fourteen difficult winding miles. The canoes were now almost useless—the men were becoming very demoralized—they wanted horses. At this point Sacagawea saw a high plain to the west, and recognized it as a summer retreat for her Shoshone tribe. This gave all of the men another morale boost—her people had horses. (Note 4)

Note 1. Stephen Ambrose, *Undaunted Courage,* (New York, Simon and Schuster, 1996), Pages 249-250

Note 2, Ibid, Page 255.

Note 3, Ibid, Pages 257-259.

Note 4, Ibid, Pages 261-262.

CHAPTER 57

Captain Lewis Finds the Source of the Missouri River

After much discussion, the captains decided to send a small party up the nearby Rocky Mountains. Although Captain Clark wanted to lead the party very badly, he had been ill and his feet were in bad shape—from prickly pears going through his moccasins. He also had a tumor on his ankle.

Thus it was decided that Captain Clark would stay with the men, the supplies, and the boats. Captain Lewis would proceed west with Drewer—the great hunter and sign-talker, and Privates Shields and McNeal. The Captains decided not to send Sacagawea since she was still recovering from her illness—and would slow the men down with a baby on her back. Besides, she would be needed later to help the Corps of Discovery bargain with her people for horses.

As Captain Lewis and his men followed the Jefferson/Missouri River, they went four miles up a mountain on August 12, 1805. Here they found a cold stream flowing from the Rocky Mountains—the source of the mighty Missouri River. As they drank from the stream, Private McNeal stood with one foot on each side of the Missouri—something he would want to tell his heirs about. (Note 1)

The men continued up the mountain, went through the Lemhi Pass, and now saw the other side of the continental divide. Meriwether Lewis could now see more immense mountains to the west—with snow on their peaks—in mid August. Now Captain Lewis knew that

President Jefferson's hope for a Northwest Passage by water was just a naïve dream. (Note 2)

After going down the west side of the mountain about three quarters of a mile, the men found a creek flowing west. Captain Lewis thought it was the beginning of the Columbia River—he wasn't too far off. It was actually the Clearwater River, which flows into the Snake River, which eventually flows into the Columbia River coming in from the north.

These discoveries were important to the mission, but their immediate need was horses. They had seen traces of Indians, but no Shoshones were yet to be found.

Note 1, Stephen Ambrose, *Undaunted Courage,* (New York, Simon and Schuster, 1996), Page 266.

Note 2, Ibid, Pages 266-267.

CHAPTER 58
Wheeling and Dealing with the Shoshones

Finally on August 13, 1805, Captain Lewis, Drouillard, and the two privates came upon a Shoshone war party of sixty warriors—led by their chief—Cameahwait (pronounced "Ca-me`-ah-wait"). The Indians were out searching for their enemies—the Blackfeet, who had recently attacked the Shoshones. Cameahwait and his men were suspicious of the white men, thinking that they might be spies for, or allies of the Blackfeet. (Note 1)

Using "Drewer" to use his sign-talking skills, Captain Lewis somewhat allayed the Indians' fears. He did an abbreviated "dog and pony show", and gave the Indians trinkets, mirrors, and an American flag.

Cameahwait then invited the Americans to the main Shoshone camp, and allowed them to stay in a teepee. Since the Americans and the Shoshones had very little food, the next day Cameahwait allowed Drouillard to hunt for deer. He did, however, send some braves to follow the hunter to make sure that he did not run away. The Indians were still suspicious of the Americans' motives. Drouillard the great hunter, eventually killed three deer and gave all of them to the hungry Shoshones. This act helped to improve American/Indian relations. (Note 2)

As relations became more relaxed, Captain Lewis began telling Cameahwait about the Corps of Discovery and the American mission west. Cameahwait volunteered the information that there was an old man in the tribe who had been west—over all of the mountains. This, of course, interested the Americans very much.

On August 16, Captain Lewis invited Cameahwait and his men to the Corps of Discovery camp, near the forks of the Jefferson/Missouri River. There the chief could meet his Co-captain Clark, and a large black man. Lewis also told the chief that Clark had a Shoshone woman with him named Sacagawea. This name apparently did not ring a bell with Cameahwait—or the now famous name was lost in the translation. The Indians were curious enough to proceed, but were still leery about a Blackfeet trap. (Note 3)

Note 1, Stephen Ambrose, *Undaunted Courage,* (New York, Simon and Schuster, 1996), Page 269.

Note 2, Ibid, Page 275.

Note 3, Ibid, Page 276.

CHAPTER 59

Sacagawea Saves the Mission—Again

Early on August 16, 1805, the four Americans, the Shoshones, and a few extra horses set out for the main camp of the Corps of Discovery—near the forks of the Missouri River. As they drew closer, the Indians became suspicious again—thinking that they were being led into a Blackfeet trap.

In a gutsy move, Captain Lewis gave Chief Cameahwait his tri-corner hat and his rifle. He also had his three men give their hats and rifles to the Indians—to emphasize the Americans' friendliness. (Note 1)

When night came, and there was still no Captain Clark, the Shoshones became suspicious again of Captain Lewis' motives. At this point Cameahwait agreed to allow Drouillard and one brave to bring this Captain Clark from their main camp the next morning. Drewer left at dawn, and soon accomplished his mission. At about 9:00 A. M. an Indian scout reported that there white men coming.

Soon the two parties met near the three forks of the Missouri. Cameahwait gave Captain Clark the Shoshone hug—by rubbing faces and putting shells in his hair—just as he had done with Captain Lewis. This was certainly not fun for the Captains to have grease paint on their faces and shells in their hair, but it was certainly better than an arrow or a bullet in the back. No doubt some of the men of the mission had trouble holding back a smile or a laugh—seeing their brave leaders being made honorary Indians.

As this ritual was going on, a Shoshone girl named Jumping Fish recognized Sacagawea, and the two teens began hugging, crying and talking. Jumping Fish had gotten her name as she jumped a stream to avoid being captured by the Hidatsas. Sacagawea, of course, had not been so fortunate.

That afternoon the Captains set up camp north of the three forks—a sight later to be known in Montana as Camp Fortunate. Lewis also had one of the boats' large sails put up as a canopy for their powwow.

But soon communication was not going well—as might be expected. Lewis decided to dispense with Drouillard's hand signals, and set up a communication chain as follows: Sacagawea would talk to her Shoshone people, and translate the words to Charbonneau in Hidatsa; he would then translate the words to Private Labiche in French; the private would then translate the words to the Captains in English.

Just as this cumbersome process started, Sacagawea began staring at Cameahwait. Then, like a scene from a Hollywood "B" movie, she recognized him as her long lost brother. Perhaps it was luck, or divine intervention, but the Captains idea to take Sacagawea on the mission had certainly paid off. (Note 2)

The conference was interrupted, as Sacagawea ran to her brother, embraced him, and cried for joy. As the council continued, there were no more suspicions of the white men's motives, as Sacagawea told her people of the doctoring and kindnesses of the Captains, and the men of the mission. Perhaps Cameahwait was also pleased to see his young nephew Pomp for the first time.

Note 1, Stephen Ambrose, *Undaunted Courage,*(New York, Simon and Schuster, 1996), Page 276.
Note 2, Ibid, Page 277.

CHAPTER 60

Living with the Shoshones— and Bargaining for Horses

As the Corps of Discovery settled into a routine at Camp Fortunate near the base of the mountains, Cameahwait told the Captains of the Salmon River—which might feed into the Columbia River. Thus, Captain Clark was sent with eleven men to explore this possibility. If the Salmon proved navigable, the men would not need many horses.

At the same time, Captain Lewis stayed at Camp Fortunate to trade for horses with the Shoshones. He also needed to pack their supplies for the portage up the mountain, and through the Lemhi Pass to Cameahwait's village—just on the other side of the Continental Divide. Lewis also had twenty wooden saddles made by breaking up boxes and cutting off paddles—in case the water route did not work.

On August 20, a large party of over fifty Shoshones came to Camp Fortunate. After a council was held and some presents were given to the Indians, Lewis realized how starved these people were. With very few weapons at their disposal, the Shoshones had to live in the mountains for survival from their enemies. The area was, however, not good for hunting or growing food. In the next few days Captain Lewis and his eighteen men caught many fish, and killed a number of deer to feed the poor hungry Indians.

By August 26, 1805, the entire party made it up the mountain, and through the Lemhi Pass to Cameahwait's village on the Lemhi/ Salmon River. Captain Clark was already camped down river, but had left a note—the Salmon River is impassible. Thus, the men would need many horses for the land route over the rest of the mountains.

Brother or not, Cameahwait was not going to give his horses to the Corps of Discovery. He and his braves for the most part drove a hard bargain for each horse. For one thing the Shoshones needed horses for the upcoming buffalo hunt. They had also lost horses to the Blackfeet. At one point Captain Clark had to trade his pistol, his knife, and one hundred rounds of ammunition for one horse. (Note 1)

In Any case by the end of August of 1805, the Corps of Discovery was ready to head over the many mountains to come. They had bought twenty-nine horses from the Shoshones. Unfortunately for the Corps of Discovery, the horses were the castoffs of the herd. (Note 2).

In a last gesture of friendship to the Captains, Cameahwait agreed to allow Old Toby and two of his sons to go with the mission to lead them across the mountain ranges to the Columbia River. Perhaps it was because his sister Sacagawea decided to go west with the Corps of Discovery.

How ironic is it that after only a two week reunion with her Shoshone people, that Sacagawea wanted to go on with the expedition. Lewis and Clark had no further use for her, since she had never been west of her tribe's village. Perhaps it was due to her "husband" Charbonneau's insistence—because he wanted to be paid for the entire trip. It could also have been that the Captains had become attached to her, and/ or considered her part of the mission. This should have been an easy decision for them.

Note 1, Stephen Ambrose, *Undaunted Courage,* (New York, Simon and Schuster, 1996), Page 283.

Note 2, James P. Ronda, *Lewis and Clark Among the Indians,*(Lincoln, University of Nebraska Press, 1984), Page 154

Chapter 61

Over the Bitterroot Mountains— to the Columbia River

On September 1, 1805, the Corps of Discovery started over the Bitterroot Mountains. This phase of the trip would turn out to be the most difficult part of the journey. The area is still basically uninhabited two hundred years later.

On September 3rd, the men saw snow on the distant mountains. On September 4th, the mission was fortunate to come upon the Salish Indians, who were allies of the Shoshones—and on their way to join their brothers for the buffalo hunt. Probably due to the presence of Old Toby and Sacagawea, the Salish acted friendly toward the white men. They were a tribe of four hundred people, and had five hundred horses. This time the Captains were able to buy thirteen horses for a few trinkets. The Corps of Discovery now had thirty-nine horses, one mule, and three colts—to be used as food in an emergency. (Note 1)

On September 16th, the mission was almost stymied by six to eight inches of snow. They kept pushing on, but were near their breaking point, due to hunger and fatigue.

The Captains decided to send Clark ahead with six hunters, to find and leave food along the trail for the rest of the mission. Captain Clark did his job well as usual. By September 20th Clark was out of the mountains, and had met up with the friendly Nez-Perce' Indians. The Nez-Perce' gave Clark some dried fish and some roots, to send back to the starving main body of the expedition. The men were reunited on

September 22, after one of the greatest forced marches in American history. (Note 2)

Why were the Nez-Perce' Indians friendly to the white men? When Captain Clark and his six hungry hunters ate real food furnished by the Nez-Perce', they gorged themselves and became very sick and weak. It would have been easy for the Indians to have wiped out the white men and taken their weapons and supplies. Here again, an Indian woman saved the lives of the men. Her name was Watkuweis (meaning returned from a far country). Just like Sacagawea, she had been captured—this time by Blackfeet—but later sold to a white trader and treated well, before making her way back home. Watkuweis told the Nez-Perce' that the white men meant them no harm. (Note 3)

The chief of the Nez-Perce'—Twisted Hair told the Captains that they were only five "sleep-overs" to the Columbia River, and five more to the falls of the Columbia. This, of course, was great news to the men of the mission. The chief also showed the Captains a nearby creek which lead to the Clearwater River—which would lead to the Columbia River. (Actually the Clearwater would lead to the Snake River, which would then lead to the Columbia River—coming in from the north).

Captain Clark then found some ponderosa pine trees, that he had the healthier men fell and make into canoes. This time he had to use the Indian method of burning out the insides, since their supply of sharp axes had been greatly depleted—for use as gifts to the various Indian tribes.

Chief Twisted Hair volunteered to keep and care for the horses of the Corps of Discovery—to be used in the spring of 1806 on the return trip east. Captain Clark wisely had the horses branded.

On October 7, 1805, the men loaded the four large and one small dugout canoes, and started down the swift Clearwater River. Although the captains and most of the men were still weak from various illnesses, their spirits were lifted—they were going down-stream for the first time since they left the Ohio River at Louisville, Kentucky two years ago. (Note 4)

As the boats continued down the Clearwater, the men started to encounter some rapids. At this point Old Toby left—without being paid for his work guiding the mission. He was apparently afraid of running the rapids, or meeting with enemy Indians.

On October 10th, the canoes reached the Snake River coming in from the south. With the hunting and fishing getting better, the men's health was improving also. On October 16, 1805, the mission finally came upon the Columbia River—coming in from the north. (Note 5)

As the Corps of Discovery continued down the Columbia River, they began to interact with more Indians. They started trading and getting information about the soon to be encountered rapids and falls. On October 23, the mission reached the falls of the Columbia River—a fifty-five mile long section of the river. By canoeing and some portages, they reached the end of the falls by the end of October. At times the captains even had to hire Indians and their horses to carry their canoes and supplies down river.

After another difficult portage on November 1 and 2, the Corps of Discovery was now in a more navigable part of the Columbia. The terrain also changed, with many trees along the banks, and migrating waterfowl everywhere. More and more Indians came to visit the men—mostly to trade, but usually drove a hard bargain.

The mission was now making thirty miles a day, and nearing the Pacific Ocean. On the morning of November 7, 1805, the fog had set in. As the canoes continued down the Columbia, the sky cleared that afternoon. The Corps of Discovery was still thirty-four miles away, but could see a small part of their final objective—the Pacific Ocean. We don't know what Sacagawea or Meriwether Lewis, or the men said, but Captain William Clark's famous saying (now on a U. S. nickel, but quoted incorrectly) in his field notes was scribbled: "Ocian in view! O! the joy!". They were now 4,142 miles from the mouth of the Missouri River, and had been gone from their Camp Wood there for over seventeen months. (Note 6)

Note1, Stephen Ambrose, *Undaunted Courage,* (New York, Simon and Schuster, 1996), Page 290.

Note 2, Ibid, Page 298.

Note 3, Ibid, Page 300.

Note 4, Ibid, Page 301.

Note 5, Ibid, Page 304.

Note 6, Ibid, Page 310.

CHAPTER 62
A Rainy West Coast Winter—at Fort Clatsop

As the Corps of Discovery continued toward the Pacific Ocean, they set up camp on November 10, 1805—on the north bank of the Columbia River. They were now less than ten miles from the Pacific/ mouth of the Columbia River. They became trapped for a week by high wind, the waves, and the tide. It also rained for eleven days. What had been a joyous occasion turned into days of misery with wet clothes on, difficulty to keep their fires lighted, and very little food. The friendly Clatsop Indians crossed the raging Columbia River to trade for food. The Captains were very impressed with the Indians' navigating skills, and their more reasonable trading demands. (Note 1)

The men continued searching for a suitable winter campsite north of the Columbia River until November 25, when they moved back up the Columbia—to cross to the south bank on a calmer part of the river. After crossing to the south bank, they explored a number of campsites until December 7, 1805 (America's first important December 7).

At this point the Captains apparently could not decide which area would be best. In an unusual moment in a military mission, Lewis and Clark opted for a democratic vote. They let all of the men vote, and included York—William Clark's slave, and Sacagawea. As far as it is known in America, this is the first time that an African-American man and a woman—much less a slave and a Native American were allowed to vote for anything. It seems obvious that William Clark was friendlier with Sacagawea than was Meriwether Lewis, since he nicknamed her Jane. During the voting, Clark noted in his journal: "Janey in favor of a place where there is plenty of potas" (edible roots). (Note 2)

They voted to stay on an inlet near the Pacific Ocean for the winter—hoping that a trade vessel would come by to replenish their meager supplies, and possibly take them home by boat. They named the winter camp Fort Clatsop for the nearby friendly Indians, and built log huts for all members of the Corps of Discovery. Christmas was celebrated in an austere fashion, but some presents were exchanged. Sacagawea gave Captain Clark two dozen white weasel tails. This gift was at times considered romantic as a Shoshone custom. On November 30th, Sacagawea had also given a hungry Captain Clark a small piece of bread that she had been hoarding. We also know that Clark rebuked Charbonneau at least once for striking his wife. (Note 3)

Perhaps this was another star-crossed romance—similar to brother George Rogers Clark's romance with the Spanish Princess—Teresa de Leyba. We will never know, but the weasel tales seem to show up in the famous portrait of Meriwether Lewis in Indian dress—apparently a later gift from William Clark. Sacagawea also got to go with Captain Clark to see a beached whale that he had found on January 6, 1806.

As the miserable rainy winter continued, the Captains at least got to catch up with their paperwork. Captain Lewis continued his wonderfully detailed descriptions and sketches of flora, fauna, fish, and animals. Captain Clark made another accurately detailed map of the western part of the continent—from Fort Mandan on the Missouri River to the Pacific Ocean. Along with Clarks map from St. Louis to Fort Mandan, the two maps became invaluable to define the American west. There are some indications that Captain Lewis also helped with the map. After all, both captains did a lot of exploring—in different areas most of the time. (Note 4)

As the rainy winter continued at Fort Clatsop food became more scarce, and more people were ill than had been in the very cold winter of 1805 at Fort Mandan. When do we leave asked the men? When the mountain snows are passable answered the captains!

Note 1, Stephen Ambrose, *Undaunted Courage,* (New York, Simon and Schuster, 1996), Page 313.

Note 2, Ibid, Page 316.

Note 3, Ibid, Page 438.

Note 4, Ibid, Page 331.

Chapter 63

First Leg East—Back to the Nez-Perce'

As spring slowly began to come at Fort Clatsop in 1806, all members of the Corps of Discovery were very anxious to start the journey east. No ship came to take the men back, so they must now retrace their steps east toward St. Louis.

Captain Lewis was anxious to get back to Washington, and make his trip report to his boss President Jefferson—even though some of it would be bad news. Captain Clark was anxious to return to his relatives in Kentucky, and to share his adventures with big brother George, who was now fifty-four and in failing health. William Clark was also anxious to return to Virginia, to see a young lady he had met named Julia Hancock. The men of the mission were also anxious to see their families, and to receive their rewards of money and land. Charbonneau was anxious to return to Fort Mandan, get his money, and to brag about his exploits. We are not sure what Sacagawea wanted—perhaps she did not want to leave the Captains and have the adventure end.

The anticipation of returning east buoyed the spirits of the Corps, but it was going to be no picnic. The difficult falls of the Columbia and Missouri Rivers were ahead, and the nasty Bitterroot Mountains were still deep in snow. Also, as the mission left Fort Clatsop on March 23, 1806, 95 per cent of their original supplies had been depleted. This was partially due to the Clatsop's hard bargaining for canoes—which the Corps of Discovery needed to get to the falls of the Columbia River. (Note 1)

The good news was that the men now knew the route east, had buried caches of supplies in Nez-Perce' country, and also near the great falls of the Missouri. They also had their branded horses that they had left under the care of Chief Twisted Hair of the Nez-Perce'.

As the Corps of Discovery went up the Columbia River to its falls in April of 1806, they were constantly harassed by roaming Indians—mostly the Chinooks. The Indians would try to steal anything as the mission camped overnight. At one point they even stole Seaman, Captain Lewis' treasured dog. Meriwether Lewis' temper rose to the boiling point as he sent three men to retrieve the dog—with orders to kill if necessary. Knowing that they were being chased, the Indians let Seaman go and ran away—thus avoiding a possible major battle. (Note 2)

After Another difficult portage around the Celilo Falls of the Columbia River, the Captains decided to go by land to the Nez-Perce' camp—still two hundred miles away. They did have some horses and pack animals, and had bought four more horses on April 18th—but for a high price—two kettles. They all started walking, except for a private who had a severe back condition. The other nine animals were used to carry supplies. Even Sacagawea had to walk—and now with a heavier one-year-old Pomp on her back. There is no evidence that Charbonneau ever helped Sacagawea by carrying their son. (Note 3)

Fortunately for the Corps of Discovery, on April 27, 1806—after a three day march—they came upon the friendly Wallawalla Indians, and their Chief—Yellept. The Wallawallas were relatives of the Nez-Perce', and had many horses. They had fifteen lodges near what is now Walla Walla, Washington, a small town near the Oregon border. (Note 4)

Here again Sacagawea became the valuable communication link, as Chief Yellept told the Captains of a captured Shoshone woman with their tribe. The men could now again use the old communication chain: Shoshone woman to Sacagawea; she to Charbonneau in Hidatsa; he in French to Drouillard or Labiche, and then to the Captains in English. This became the first direct talks with Indians—other than sign language—since the mission had left the Shoshones in the fall of 1805. (Note 5)

After some more difficult trading for horses (Captain Lewis even had to give up his personal dueling pistol), the Corps of Discovery was ready to continue east. They now had twenty-three excellent horses. As the mission left the friendly Wallawallas on April 30, 1806, Chief Wellept told the Captains of a land route south of the Snake River to the Nez-Perce' camp. This shortcut would save them eighty miles. The Corps of Discovery was glad to take his suggestion.

After four days of riding and marching in bad weather and their food running out, the mission met some roving Nez-Perce' Indians. The Corps of Discovery arrived back at Chief Twisted Hair's village on May 4, 1806. (Note 6)

Note 1, Stephen Ambrose, *Undaunted Courage,* (New York, Simon and Schuster, 1996), Page 353.

Note 2, Ibid, Page 355.

Note 3, Ibid, Page 357.

Note 4, Ibid, Page 358.

Note 5, Ibid, Page 358.

Note 6, Ibid, Page 359.

CHAPTER 64

Over the Snowy Bitterroot Mountains— With the Nez-Perce' to the Rescue

As the Corps of Discovery became re-acquainted with their Nez-Perce' friends in early May of 1806, they were still anxious to move east. By May 7th they could see much winter snow still left on the Bitterroot Mountains. The Nez-Perce' told the Captains that the mountains would not be passable until early June. (Note 1)

Captain Clark kept busy by becoming the doctor this time. He would merely rub linament on the Indians' various ailments, and as some became cured he became their hero. He used this skill to trade for food for the men.

Captain Lewis kept busy rounding up the mission's horses. Chief Twisted Hair had not done a very good job caring for the horses—only twenty-one horses and ten saddles were recovered.

To kill time the Captains impressed the Nez-Perce' by doing an expanded "dog and pony show"—showing the Indians a magnet, a spyglass, a watch, and shooting Meriwether Lewis' amazing and silent air gun. The men had horse races with the Nez-Perce', but lost as usual.

With the nearby Clearwater River rising due to melting snow, the Captains decided to start for the mountains. After a farewell party on June 8, 1806, the Corps of Discovery left the friendly Nez-Perce' and started east again. On June 15th as the men started up the mountains, spring turned into winter within a few hours—with the snow eight to ten feet deep. Since the snow was firm enough to support the horses, the

Corps of Discovery continued on. On the next day the snow became twelve to fifteen feet deep, and there was no grass for the horses—a recipe for disaster! (Note 2)

With no one to guide them, the Captains wisely decided to go back down the mountain. They also sent their faithful scout "Drewer" back to the Nez-Perce' to hire a guide. By June 21st the men went further away from the mountain to hunt for food.

On June 23rd Drewer arrived back at camp with three Nez-Perce' guides. He had given the Indians two rifles to get them to agree to be guides. The Captains had authorized Drewer to do this as a last resort. It turned out to be a good bargain, since the young braves—not yet twenty—were great guides. They knew all of the valleys in the mountains where there was no snow, and thus grass for the horses. (Note 3)

On June 27th the Corps of Discovery started up the mountains again—this time led by their young guides. By June 30th the mission was out of the snow—and over the Bitterroot Mountains. They soon reached their old camp where they had stayed in September of 1805 that the Captains had named—Traveler's Rest. No doubt the people of the mission were ready for some rest.

Note 1, Stephen Ambrose, *Undaunted Courage,* (New York, Simon and Schuster, 1996), Page 360.

Note 2, Ibid, Page 371.

Note 3, Ibid, Page 374.

CHAPTER 65

A Bold and Dangerous Plan—to Split the Mission into Five Parts

As the Corps of Discovery relaxed at Travelers Rest in early July of 1806, the Captains finalized their bold exploration plan. It would go as follows:

1. Captain Lewis with nine men and seventeen horses would go overland to the falls of the Missouri. There he would leave three men to dig up their cache of supplies, portage the falls, and rejoin Lewis later. Captain Lewis and the six men would go north to explore the Marias River, and then rejoin the men doing the portage below the falls of the Missouri. By this route Lewis hoped to meet with the Blackfeet Indians and give his standard American speech;

2. Captain Clark with the rest of the Corps of Discovery would go by land back to Camp Fortunate, where they had left their canoes. At this point they would descend the nearby Jefferson/Missouri River about one hundred miles back to the three forks of the Missouri. Here Captain Clark would order Sergeant Ordway and ten men to continue down the Missouri to the falls, and help with the portage. They would then meet up with Captain Lewis' group coming in from their northern exploration;

3. Captain Clark, with the remaining ten men plus York, Charbonneau, Sacagawea, and Pomp, would go by land for approximately fifty miles east to meet the Yellowstone River—coming in from the south. Here they would make canoes, go down the Yellowstone to its junction with the Missouri, and rejoin the rest of the mission. Before leaving in canoes, Captain Clark was to dispatch Sergeant Pryor and two men to go by land to the Mandan villages with some horses—to use for trading, and some as gifts—to hopefully ensure a welcome home for the Corps of Discovery. Although this was still a 450 mile trip, it was much shorter than the winding water routes. (Note 1)

The plan was both bold and dangerous, with the warlike Blackfeet and other Indians nearby—and the Corps of Discovery to be split into five small parts. In any case, all of the men were soon briefed and ready to go—showing their faith and trust in their two great leaders. Captain Lewis' part of the journey would be nearly eight hundred miles, while Captain Clarks part would be about one thousand miles. As the men separated on July 3, 1806, they confidently said to each other—see you at the junction (of the Missouri and Yellowstone Rivers) in five or six weeks. (Note 2)

Note 1, Stephen Ambrose, *Undaunted Courage,* (New York, Simon and Schuster, 1996), Page 376.
Note 2, Ibid, Page 379.

CHAPTER 66

Captain Clark's Pleasure Cruise

The Corps of Discovery left Traveler's Rest on July 3, 1806,—split into two parts. Captain Lewis with his nine men, seventeen horses, and five Nez-Perce' guides headed east by land toward the falls of the Missouri. Captain Clark with the rest of the mission headed south by land through the mountains.

By July 8th Captain Clark had reached their old Camp Fortunate—at the base, and east of the mountains—where they retrieved their hidden canoes. Now traveling by water on the Jefferson/Missouri River, they soon reached the now named Three Forks of the Missouri. Here Captain Clark dispatched Sargeant Ordway and his ten men to continue down the Missouri to help Lewis' men portage the falls, and meet later as planned.

William Clark and his part of the mission headed east by land. Sacagawea again proved to be invaluable by guiding them through the Bozeman Mountain pass to the Yellowstone River. Upon arriving at the river on July 15th, Clark soon found some large trees, and built two twenty-eight foot long canoes—long but narrow and shallow (16 to 24" wide and 16 to 18" deep). He then decided to tie the canoes together for stability. Compared to most other parts of the exploration, Captain Clark's trip down the Yellowstone River was now like a pleasure cruise—with only fourteen people and a baby in two large canoes. There were also many buffalo near the river to use for food. (Note 1)

The only downside of the trip was that soon some sneaky Crow Indians stole half of his fifty horse herd that was following the canoes. Captain Clark then decided to send Sergeant Pryor and three men to take the balance of the horses down the river, and then to the Mandan villages as planned—to be used for gifts and trading. Unfortunately, the Crows soon stole these horses also. The resourceful sergeant did manage to make two bull boats, and rejoined Clark on the Missouri River on August 8th (a bull boat is a small boat made by stretching the skin of a bull buffalo over a frame of flexible sticks). The valuable upside of the trip was Captain Clark's accurate map of the area—adding more information about the American west. (Note 2)

Captain Clark's part of the trip now went even faster—with only ten people and a baby in his two large canoes—and, of course going down stream. Clark even had time to carve his name on a rock formation by the river, and name it Pompey's Tower in honor of Sacagawea's son—who he now called "my boy Pomp". (Note 3)

There is no evidence that Charbonneau was jealous of Captain Clark's affection for his wife and his son. After all, he had more squaws back at Fort Mandan, and could buy more with the money he would soon get.

As the trip continued to go smoothly, the canoes arrived at the junction of the Missouri on August 3, 1806. Clark had gone one almost a thousand miles in one month. Since there was no sign of the rest of the mission, he set up camp to wait. Since the mosquitoes were very plentiful and there was very little game to hunt for food, Clark decided to go down river. After leaving Lewis a note on a pole by the Missouri, his part of the mission found a suitable camp about fifty miles down the Missouri River. This camp would later be named Point of Reunion. (Note 4)

Note 1, Bernard De Voto, *The Journals of Lewis and Clark,* (New York, Houghton Mifflin Company, 1953), Page 449.

Note 2, Ibid, Page 450.

Note 3, Ibid, Page 451.

Note 4, Stephanie Ambrose Tubbs with Clay Straus Jenkinson, *The Lewis and Clark Companion,* (New York, Henry Holt and Company, LLC, 2003), Page319.

Chapter 67

Captain Lewis' Nightmare Journey

Captain Lewis' part of the split exploration was mostly a series of problems. On the second day out, the three Nez-Perce' guides decided to go back home—fearing contact with their enemies—the Blackfeet and the Hidatsas. Lewis was very sorry to see the fine young men go, since they had become good friends and were extremely valuable to the mission. Unfortunately the Nez-Perce' would be treated badly in the future by white American settlers—as were most Native-Americans.

As Captain Lewis' group continued east, a roving band of Indians—probably Blackfeet—stole half of his horses. By July 13th, Lewis reached the upper portage of the falls of the Missouri. Now, with only six horses for his nine men, Lewis found it necessary to leave at least six men at the falls. At least this would supply more men to help with the long portage, and unload the cache of supplies and the white pirogue—which had been left at the base of the falls. Sergeant Ordway and his ten men had not yet arrived.

Still determined to explore the Marias River area to the north, Lewis picked Drouillard/Drewer and the two Field brothers to go with him. As the men started north on July 16th, they began to see many signs of Indians. They explored the Marias River north to within thirty miles of the present day American border with Canada.

On July 26th Lewis sent Drewer down to a nearby valley where he had spotted some horses. He soon saw some thirty horses on a ridge overlooking the valley. Using his telescope, Captain Lewis saw Indians on some of the horses—watching Drouillard. Lewis then bravely made contact with the Indians, and waved Drouillard—the great sign talker—back to interpret.

The Indians turned out to be Blackfeet—eight young braves who were part of a large hunting party. Lewis gave the Indians a medal, a flag, and a hanky. All of the men smoked Drouillard's peacepipe, and the Indians suggested that the two groups camp together for the night. (Note 1)

Since relations seemed to be going well, Lewis and his men bedded down for the night. After Captain Lewis kept watch over their supplies and horses until 11:30, he woke Reubin Field to take over. Unfortunately, Reubin soon fell asleep again. At first light three Indians stole all four rifles from the sleeping Americans. Drouillard awoke first, alerted the others, and chased the Indian who had his rifle. After a wrestling match, Drewer got his rifle back. The Field brothers chased the Indian who had both of their rifles. After more wrestling, Reubin Field stabbed the Indian with his knife. As the Indian died, the brothers retrieved their rifles. (Note 2)

Captain Lewis chased the Indian who had his rifle, pulled his horse pistol, and motioned to the Indian to lay down his rifle. The Indian complied, but then helped other Blackfeet to steal the Americans' horses. As one Indian turned his musket toward Lewis, the Captain shot the Indian in the belly. Not dead yet, the Indian fired a shot at Captain Lewis—barely missing his head. This tragic incident was now over, as the young braves retreated—back to their large band of Blackfeet brothers. (Note 3)

Lewis and his men soon rounded up three of their original horses, and four of the Indian's horses. They quickly burned everything that the Indians had left—bows, arrows, etc. After rapidly packing their supplies, the men headed south as fast as possible.

Captain Lewis' part of the mission was now in grave danger of being wiped out—by the nearby large band of now very hostile Blackfeet Indians. Lewis now had also put his other men at the falls of the Missouri in harms' way. Sergeant Ordway and his ten men, and/or the six the captain had left at the upper portage would be no match for a band of almost two hundred Blackfeet on the warpath.

To avoid a total disaster, Captain Lewis and his three men rode southeast toward the lower portage of the falls of the Missouri. By taking only two breaks to rest the horses, the men had ridden one hundred miles—from 3:30 A. M. on July 27 to 2:00 A. M. on July 28. Feeling safer now, Lewis and his very tired men and horses rested until dawn. After riding another twelve miles, the men were pleased to see the Missouri River—below the falls. (Note 4)

After riding eight miles down the side of the Missouri, Lewis heard rifles being fired on the river. As they got to the river bank they saw their flagship—the white pirogue—and five canoes. When they pulled over, Captain Lewis quickly explained the situation. The men loaded Lewis' supplies, set the horses free, and the combined force continued down the Missouri. After going downstream another fifteen miles, the men decided it was safe to make camp—but on the south side of the Missouri, away from a possible Blackfeet attack.

The combined forces now had Captain Lewis and his original nine men, plus Sergeant Ordway and his ten men. They were anxious to meet Captain Clark and his group at the junction of the Yellowstone and Missouri Rivers.

Captain Lewis' flotilla continued uneventfully down the Missouri River. As they passed the mouth of the Marias River, the men picked up more supplies that had been left in a cache in the summer of 1805. On August 7, 1806, Lewis and his men reached the junction of the Yellowstone and Missouri Rivers—where they found Clark's note.

As they continued toward Clark's camp on August 11, Captain Lewis saw some elk near some willow trees. Lewis and Private Cruzatte went ashore to hunt. After killing one elk, the two men split up and went into the woods to look for more elk. Now, another bad situation for Captain Lewis—he was hit by a bullet in his buttocks. In severe pain, he called for Private Cruzatte. When the private did not answer, Lewis started toward the boats, and yelled at the men to prepare for a possible Indian attack. As Lewis painfully made it back to the boats, there were no more shots. Lewis then sent a party of men out to look for Private Cruzatte—still wary of Indians. When they soon returned with the private, he denied shooting Captain Lewis. The bullet was found in Lewis' leather breeches, a .54 caliber—used only in U. S. Army rifles. It was obviously a sad accident as Private Cruzatte had mistaken the Captain for an elk in the willows. (Note 5)

After dressing Captain Lewis' wound, he was placed on his stomach in the white pirogue—what an embarrassment for the co-leader of the Corps of Discovery. The boats then continued down river, and the men were very happy to find Captain Clark's group on the next day—August 12, 1806—at the camp soon to be called Point of Reunion. (Note 6)

Upon hearing of his friend's injury, Clark rushed to his side. Lewis assured Clark that the wound was not serious, and that he would be well in three or four weeks. The rest of the men were in good health, good spirits, and anxious to return to the Mandans, then get back to St. Louis.

Note 1, Stephen Ambrose, *Undaunted Courage,* (New York, Simon and Schuster, 1996), Page 388.

Note 2, Ibid, Page 391.

Note 3, Ibid, Page 391.

Note 4, Ibid, Page 394.

Note 5, Bernard De Voto, *The Journals of Lewis and Clark,* (New York, Houghton Mifflin Company, 1953), Pages 445-446.

Note 6, Ibid, Page 447.

CHAPTER 68
Back to the Mandan Villages

After two more easy days of rowing with the current, the Corps of Discovery arrived at the Mandan villages on August 14, 1806. There were friendly reunions with the Mandans—particularly Chief Black Cat, Chief She-heke ("Big White"), and Hidatsa Chief Le Borgne ("One Eye"). There were hugs, presents, pipe smoking, and councils. Poor Captain Lewis did not participate since he was still in much pain from his incident. (Note 1)

Captain Clark attempted to get the chiefs to go with the Corps of Discovery to Washington to meet with their new "great white father"—President Thomas Jefferson. At first the Indians declined, being afraid of the warlike Sioux to the south. Finally Big White agreed to go, but only if his entourage went also. This consisted of Big White's wife and their son. It also included his interpreter Jessaume and his Indian wife. The Captains agreed reluctantly, knowing that this scenario might overload their boats.

Before leaving for St. Louis on August 17, 1806, Clark settled with Charbonneau. He received $500.331/3 for his horse, his teepee, and his services. Poor Sacagawea got nothing! (Note 2)

Obviously William Clark had great respect, admiration, and possibly a romantic interest in Sacagawea, as he offered to take her son Jean Baptiste to St. Louis—to raise as his own son. She said maybe next summer, after he has been weaned. In a letter to Charbonneau of August 20, 1806, Clark paid tribute to Sacagawea, referring to her as "your woman who accompanied you on that long dangerous and fatigueing rout to the Pacific Ocian and back diserved a greater reward for her attention and services on that rout than we had in our power to give her". (Note 3)

It was obviously an emotional parting, as Lewis and Clark and his men of the Corps of Discovery left the Mandan villages—where they had spent the winter of 1805 with their new friends.

Another interesting event happened as the mission prepared to start south. Private Coulter requested permission to leave the Corps of Discovery and go back up the Yellowstone River with two men from Kentucky—who had recently joined the exploration. The captains granted his wish. He would become America's first mountain man, and later discover Yellowstone Park. (Note 4)

Note 1, Stephen Ambrose, *Undaunted Courage,* (New York, Simon and Schuster, 1996), Page 398.

Note 2, Ibid, Page 399.

Note 3, Ibid, Page 399.

Note 4, Ibid, Page 399.

CHAPTER 69
The Triumphant Return to St. Louis

As the Corps of Discovery left the Mandan villages on August 17, 1806, they were still about sixteen hundred miles from St. Louis by way of the Missouri River. Captain Lewis was still on his belly in the white pirogue, since his wound was still too painful for him to walk.

The mission soon passed the friendly Arikara villages, and continued to make good time downstream—now making seventy to eighty miles per day. By August 22nd, Captain Lewis was able to walk a little. (Note 1)

The men were still worried about facing their enemies the Teton Sioux. Now they had only canoes and rifles—not a keelboat with cannons. On August 31st, the Corps of Discovery heard gunshots nearby. Fortunately they soon met up with some friendly Yankton Sioux Indians—just out for target practice. As they exchanged greetings and information, the captains found out that a Yankton Sioux chief had gone to Washington—their first good Indian news since they left the Nez-Perce'. There were no more contacts with Indians for the rest of the trip. (Note 2)

On September 3rd, the canoes met a trader from St. Louis going upstream. The captains, of course, were hungry for news from civilization. They were relieved to hear that the boss—Thomas Jefferson had been re-elected. They were not thrilled to hear that General Wilkinson was now governor of the Louisiana Territory. Yes, this was the same egotistical ambitious man who had helped to undermine George Rogers Clark's stellar career.

The next day they reached what was now called Floyd's Bluff—near present day Sioux City, Iowa. The men all went up the hill to pay their respects at Sergeant Floyd's grave—the only American casualty of the long and dangerous mission. Miraculously, only two Indians were killed on the trip, and Captain Lewis' injury was by "friendly fire". After climbing the hill that day, Lewis was again hurting from his injury. (Note 3)

As the mission continued toward St. Louis, they ran into another trading boat—owned by their friend Pierre Chouteau. The Captains bought a gallon of whiskey from the traders (with promise to pay Chouteau in St. Louis), and gave each man a dram of the spirits. The canoes soon met more traders and got food and whiskey—party time had begun. More good news—Captain Lewis could now walk and run. He was certainly glad that none of his friends from St. Louis had to see him on his belly in the white pirogue.

By September 15th, the Corps of Discovery reached the mouth of the Kansas River. It seemed to be a good place for a fort in the future. It is now downtown Kansas City, Missouri, about three hundred river miles from St. Louis.

The men soon met more traders with information from civilization. They found out that most Americans had given them up for dead. There were also rumors that the Corps of Discovery had been captured by the Spanish—and killed or made into slaves, to work in Spanish gold mines. President Jefferson was very worried about the men, but felt that the "undaunted courage" of the two captains would see them through. (Note 4)

By September 18th, the boats were only one hundred fifty miles from the first settlement. At this point the men had no food, and had to live on ripe plums that they found on shore. Two days later the men were happy to see cows on the river bank—cows meant civilization. They soon got food and supplies at the villages of La Charette and St. Charles—just up the river from St. Louis.

On September 22nd, they came upon Fort Bellefontaine—built after the mission left by General Wilkinson in 1805. The captains took Big White and family to public stores at the fort and bought them clothes for their trip to Washington. (Note 5)

The next day the Corps of Discovery reached the mouth of the Missouri River. As they passed Camp Wood across the Mississippi River, they had been gone for twenty-eight months, and had gone eight thousand miles from their starting point. (Note 6)

A few miles later the Corps of Discovery reached St. Louis, with cheering crowds welcoming their hero's home. Now the parties would really start.

Note 1, Stephen Ambrose, *Undaunted Courage,* (New York, Simon and Schuster, 1996), Page 400.

Note 2, Ibid, Page 400.

Note 3, Ibid, Page 401.

Note 4, Ibid, Page 403.

Note 5, Ibid, Page 403.

Note 6, Ibid, Page 404.

CHAPTER 70

Winding Down and Partying in St. Louis

As the Corps of Discovery arrived in St. Louis on September 22, 1806, Captain Lewis was anxious to send a report to President Jefferson. Both captains were given a room at their friend's house—Pierre Chouteau. Lewis wrote a full account of the mission. They had found one hundred seventy-eight new plants, one hundred twenty-two new species of animals, and had made excellent maps of the journey. Lewis also reported the bad news—there was no Northwest Passage—just a three hundred forty mile difficult land trip between the navigable parts of the Missouri and Columbia Rivers. There were also no mammoths to be found—as President Jefferson had hoped there would be.

The first report sent, Lewis and Clark could now relax and enjoy their fame. The first formal party was held on September 25th, at Christy's Inn. As one might imagine, many questions were asked about the trip, and seventeen toasts were drunk—to President Jefferson, to Louisiana, to the enlisted men, to the captains, and so on.

As the captains continued to settle accounts with the business men of St. Louis and continue to party, their letters and reports were starting to reach the east. On October 11, 1806, their letters reached the nearest eastern newspaper—the Frankfort, Kentucky *Western World*. By October 28, the information finally reached the Pittsburg *Gazzette*, and finally the Washington *National Intelligencer* on November 3rd. Thus William Clark's family in Louisville, Kentucky received information about the trip much sooner than Meriwether Lewis' family did in Virginia. (Note 1)

In early November of 1806, the captains headed east with their entourage—Big White and his family, Sergeants Gass and Ordway, Private Labiche, Frazier, and, of course, York. The captain's friend Pierre Chouteau and some of his Osage Indian trading partners also came along. (Note 2)

Note 1, Stephen Ambrose, *Undaunted Courage,* (Ney York, Simon and Schuster, 1996), Page 412.

Note 2, Ibid, Page 417.

CHAPTER 71

William Clark Returns to His "Old Kentucky Home"

On November 9, 1806, Meriwether Lewis and William Clark reached Louisville, Kentucky—three years and one month from their first meeting there. A banquet and ball was held at William's sisters' stately manor house—Locust Grove. One can imagine the joy that was felt for the heroes who had conquered the west. (Note 1)

We can imagine the amazement on the faces of Chief Big White and his entourage, upon seeing the large second floor ballroom, and seven bedrooms at Locust Grove.

George Rogers Clark, sister Lucy, brother Jonathan, and the rest of the family were no doubt thrilled by William's triumphant return. They were hungry for information about all phases of the journey. Unfortunately, no written word seems to exist about that eventful happening. After all—it was party time at Locust Grove—still a popular site for parties and weddings.

Family and friends were certainly sad to see their heroes soon head east again. By November 13, the entourage reached Frankfort, Kentucky. Here they split into three parts. Captain Lewis, with Big White and his people would head to Monticello, in Charlottesville, Virginia—to report to President Jefferson. Pierre Chouteau and his Osage Indians would head for Washington, D. C. William Clark would head south to Fincastle, Virginia (about twenty miles north of Roanoke), to seek out Judith Hancock—a girl he had met four years ago when she was twelve. Certainly William was anxious to see her.

Was she involved with some another man? Would she even remember William Clark of Kentucky? (Note 2)

Note 1, Stephen Ambrose, *Undaunted Courage,* (New York, Simon and Schuster, 1996), Page 417.
Note 2, Ibid, Page 417.

Locust Grove-Photograph by Douglas C. Harrison

CHAPTER 72
The Courtship of Julia/Judith/Judy Hancock

When Judith Hancock was born in Fincastle, Virginia in 1791, her cousin, William Clark was twenty-one and had moved to Kentucky six years earlier. William had apparently met Judith when he was visiting his army friend William Preston, who had married Judith's sister Caroline.

A chance meeting that later turns romantic often happens in real life, and in the movies. For example, in the well done made for television mini-series, *North and South,* a Virginia gentleman—named Orey Main—happens upon a lady whose carriage had lost a wheel, and she falls into a creek. After rescuing the lady from danger, the gentleman goes off on a long military journey. After many trials and tribulations, the two people meet again, fall in love, and get married.

Clark family legend states that while William was visiting his army friend William Preston, he happened upon Judith Hancock and her cousin Harriet Kennerly. The horse that they were riding together had become nervous, and would not cross a creek. William came to the rescue, and led the horse and the women safely across the creek. Similar to Orey Main in *North and South,* William Clark goes off on a long military mission—with many trials and tribulations. This time they all meet again, and William Clark eventually marries **both women.** Truth is often stranger than fiction! (Note 1)

When William Clark arrived in Fincastle, Virginia in November of 1806, he again stayed at the estate of his friend William Preston. Here he could start courting Judith Hancock who lived nearby. William found that Judith—or Julia or Judy that she preferred—had become a lovely young lady of sixteen. She was five feet five-inches tall, with blue eyes and brown hair.

As William Clark stayed in Fincastle over Christmas of 1806, and New Years of 1807, he was enjoying a great social life with the Hancock and Preston families. It was obviously a welcome change from the bleak, cold, and rainy Christmas and New Years at Fort Clatsop in 1806. (Note 2)

At some point Julia gave William permission to ask her father for her hand. Julia's father, George Hancock, was a well-to-do Federalist, and had a number of possible reasons to deny William's request. First—William at age thirty-seven was twenty-one years older than his daughter. Second—he would hate to see his daughter move far away—to what he considered the "wilderness" of Kentucky or St. Louis. Third—George Hancock knew that William was a Jeffersonian-Republican, the opposite of his politics.

In any case, Julia's father gave his consent to their marriage. On the positive side, he would have a famous proven hero as a son-in-law, William was from another prominent Virginia family, he could probably support his daughter financially, and women usually married at a young age in early America. (Note 3)

In mid January of 1807, William Clark left Fincastle, Virginia to resume his military duties with Meriwether Lewis in Washington, D. C. His non-military mission had been accomplished!

Note 1, Jay H. Buckley, *William Clark-Indian Diplomat,* (Norman, Ok, University of Oklahoma Press, 2008), Page 251, Note 8.

Note 2, Ibid, Page 69.

Note 3, Ibid, Page 69.

CHAPTER 73
Meanwhile, Back in Eastern Virginia, And Washington, D. C.

When Meriwether Lewis and Chief Big White and his entourage arrived at Monticello in November of 1806, it was certainly a joyous occasion to meet with President Jefferson. Lewis and the President must have had an emotional reunion—after a three and a half year separation.

How did Lewis introduce the chief to the President? Did he say, Big White meet Great White (Father)? Perhaps they both found their partly common name amusing. In any case, the President and the Indian group were soon off to Washington. Jefferson was certainly anxious to show off his new western friends from the new Louisiana Territory. On December 2, 1806, Jefferson made his first proposal to Congress for compensation for the men of the Corps of Discovery. Like the Congress of modern times, they debated the issue, but did nothing.

Meriwether Lewis stayed in Virginia to party with his family and friends. He made slow progress toward Washington, as every town he passed wanted to have a dinner and a ball for him.

Captain Lewis finally made his triumphant re-entry into Washington, D. C. on December 28, 1806. He had been gone almost three years and seven months since his departure on July 5, 1803. (Note 1)

The parties continued through the end of the year, with Chief Big White and his entourage being entertained—and doing some entertaining themselves. On December 29, Lewis took the Indians to the theater. During intermission, Big White and some of the other Indians danced on the stage—what a sight that must have been for Washington theatergoers! (Note 2)

On January 1, 1807, Captain Lewis made his first formal report to President Jefferson at the White House. Although no notes were known to be taken, the two great men did go over Captain Clark's accurate map of the west. They spread the map on the floor and examined it on their hands and knees. (Note 3)

On January 14, 1807, Captain Lewis was host of the first formal ball for the Corps of Discovery. Pierre Chouteau and his Osage Indians attended, plus Big White and his group. Captain Clark was a no-show—still in Virginia courting Julia Hancock. Lewis was doing some courting also in D. C. President Jefferson was also a no-show—not wanting to upstage his protégé. Many toasts were drunk, and no doubt a good time was had by all.

As Captain Lewis moved into the White House for the winter of 1807, he and Jefferson continued to lobby Congress for equal pay for Captain Clark, and better pay for the men of the Corps of Discovery. When Clark joined Lewis in Washington on January 21, 1807, they continued to lobby together.

After a month of debate, Congress passed a bill on February 28 (by a vote of 63 to 29), giving each captain land warrants for 1,600 acres of land. The men of the mission were to get 320 acres each and also double pay. Some members of Congress objected to this lavish payout—saying that it was like taking $60,000 out of the treasury—or a lot more if the land increased in value from the current price of $2.00 per acre. (Note 4)

On the same day, President Jefferson nominated Meriwether Lewis to be governor of the Louisiana Territory. Congress approved the nomination, and Captain Lewis resigned his commission on March 2 in order to take the job. The President also tried to nominate Captain Clark for promotion to lieutenant colonel, but Secretary of War Dearborn left Clark's name off the list of promotions. This is the same guy who had squelched Clark's promotion to captain for the Corps of Discovery mission. Obviously he was not a great friend of Lewis and Clark—perhaps he felt upstaged by their fame and fortune—when technically they worked for him, since he was in charge of the military.

The President was very upset about the situation, and soon appointed Clark to Superintendent for Indian Affairs, with the rank of Brigadier General of Militia. This nomination immediately passed Congress, and General Clark started to plan his trip back to St. Louis. (Note 5)

Sergeant Pryor of the mission was promoted to ensign, and given the responsibility of getting Big White and his people back to St. Louis, and then taken back to his Mandan people. This left General Clark free to return for his new job by way of Fincastle, Virginia. Perhaps he said at the time: "I love it when a plan comes together".

Note 1, Stephen Ambrose, *Undaunted Courage,* (New York, Simon and Schuster, 1996), Page 419.

Note 2, Ibid, Page 420.

Note 3, Ibid, Page 421.

Note 4, Ibid, Page 424-425.

Note 5, Ibid, Page 426.

CHAPTER 74
Lewis and Clark—Post Mission Plans

Now that the two great men were famous, they decided to remain partners and become wealthy also. It was decided that Lewis would remain in the east to oversee the publishing of their journals and maps. At the same time Clark would go to St. Louis to start his Indian affairs job, and temporarily fill in for Lewis as Governor of the Louisiana Territory. Clark would also carry the money and land warrants for the men of the mission—who were still in St. Louis. (Note 1)

General Clark started out on his new mission on March 10, 1807. When he arrived in Fincastle, Virginia in mid March, he stayed with Julia at her parent's home. During this visit they set their wedding date—January 5, 1808. We would assume that William Clark hated to leave Julia Hancock at this point, but his new duties were calling him to St. Louis. Perhaps he said: "I'll be back in the fall to help with the wedding plans".

When General Clark arrived in St. Louis, he needed a place to stay. Perhaps he rented a room from the captains' friend Jean-Pierre Chouteau-just as had been done when the men returned from the west. He could afford to rent, but not to buy—his salary as Indian agent was only $1,500.00 per year. General Clark was kept busy working on Indian affairs, and helping to assist former acting Louisiana Territorial governor and now Secretary—Frederick Bates. One might assume that Bates was resentful of Meriwether Lewis—who was coming to take his job. Lewis was still in Philadelphia working on his personal publishing projects, and trying to run the Louisiana Territory from a long distance away. In fact, Governor Lewis was mostly busy partying in Philadelphia in the summer of 1807, and enjoying his fame as a new American hero. This fact certainly added to Secretary Bates' resentment. (Note 2)

In the fall of 1807 Governor Lewis gave General Clark permission to head east again—even though Lewis was still not in St. Louis. Lewis knew that his best friend had two missions in the east—his marriage to Julia Hancock, and a final favor for their mentor—President Thomas Jefferson. (Note 3)

Note 1, Stephen Ambrose, *Undaunted Courage,* (New York, Simon and Schuster, 1996), Page 426.

Note 2, Ibid, Pages 436-437.

Note 3, Jay H. Buckley, *William Clark-Indian Diplomat,* (Norman, Ok, University of Oklahoma Press, 2008), Page 68.

CHAPTER 75
William Clark Does a Mammoth Task

President Thomas Jefferson was often ahead of his time in his thinking. His amazing writing of The Declaration of Independence, his engineering of the Louisiana Purchase, and his guiding of its exploration, are three of his monumental accomplishments.

He was also somewhat naïve in a number of ways. For example, he was sure that there was a Northwest Passage—for a water route to the west coast. He also thought that the western Indians would become good American citizens—once they were recruited by those great captains—Lewis and Clark.

Thomas Jefferson also had a fixation that there were giant mammoths roaming the west of America. He requested that Lewis and Clark look for them, and bring back any bones or evidence of their existence. A mammoth was a large animal, similar to an elephant—but extinct long before the 1800's in America. President Jefferson had also requested that Meriwether Lewis stop at Big Bone Lick on his way to Louisville to join Clark in 1803 (now a state park on the Ohio River in Kentucky—about twenty miles southwest of Cincinnati). Earlier in 1803, a Dr. William Goforth had apparently discovered mammoth bones at this salt lick. Lewis found some bones and described a large tusk in detail in his report to Jefferson. (Note 1)

Senator John Quincy Adams, a narrow-minded Federalist, had always been against the Louisiana Purchase—saying that it was way too much money—of which we have very little—for way too much land of which we already have too much. While most people were praising President Jefferson for his successful endeavor, Adams wrote that the mission did not find any mammoths, or even any mammoth bones. (Note 2)

Thomas Jefferson, of course, was not happy being ridiculed by his Federalist adversary. Thus he requested that William Clark also make a trip to Big Bone Lick on his way back from St. Louis in the fall of 1807. First Clark must attend to his duties as Indian agent—but how could William turn down his President's request. After all, he had just been appointed brigadier general of the Upper Louisiana Militia, and principal Indian agent for all tribes west of the Mississippi River. As with every task that William Clark ever agreed to take, he dug for mammoth fossil bones diligently—but unlike Lewis or Dr. Goforth, he found none. (Note 3)

Fast forward to 2007 when a baby mammoth was found in northern Russia, who had died when she became buried in mud and apparently suffocated. That many years ago, the current twelve miles of water between northeast Russia and western Alaska were most likely a land bridge. Thus, it is possible that mammoths once roamed Alaska, Canada, and western America. Thomas Jefferson was possibly right again in his thinking—but way off in his timing.

Note 1, Stephen E. Ambrose, *Undaunted Courage*, (New York, NY, Simon & Schuster, 1996), Page 115.

Note 2, Ibid, Page 423.

Note 3, Jay H. Buckley, *William Clark-Indian Diplomat*, (Norman, Ok, University of Oklahoma Press, 2008), Page 68.

Chapter 76

William Clark's Marriage, and Meriwether Lewis' Non-marriage

In late November of 1807, Meriwether Lewis and his brother Reuben went to Fincastle, Virginia, and were invited to stay with Julia and George Hancock—William Clark's fiancé, and father-in-law to be. Clark was not there yet, but would be soon—after visiting his Kentucky relatives and reporting to President Jefferson about his lack of fossil findings.

While at the Hancock estate, Lewis met the beautiful Letitia Breckinridge and her sister Elizabeth. He was immediately smitten by Letitia, and asked to call upon her. Two days later she left for Richmond with her father—apparently to avoid Lewis' advances. Although her sister Elizabeth remained in Fincastle, Lewis showed no interest in her—perhaps brother Reuben did. (Note 1)

What happened to the love life of poor Meriwether Lewis this time? He had also failed in his courtships in Philadelphia and Washington. Did he come on too strong? Did he get drunk and make a spectacle of himself? Did he get into a political argument with Julia's father George Hancock—who was a loyal Federalist? If Lewis' hot temper started to show, it may have scared the poor girl to death. Or perhaps, Letitia did not want a man who was going to live on he edge of civilization, albeit the capitol of the new territory.

In any case a depressed Meriwether Lewis and his brother soon left for their home near Charlottesville. He apparently did not wait for his best friend to arrive. What Meriwether Lewis did or even where he stayed during the winter of 1807-1808 is unknown. (Note 2)

When William Clark reached Fincastle in December of 1807, he was no doubt disappointed that his best friend was not there. Had he asked Lewis to be his best man? In any case the thirty-seven year old William Clark, and the sixteen year old Judith Hancock were married at George Hancock's plantation Santillane near Fincastle, Virginia on January 5, 1808.

It was no doubt a beautiful wedding—with many friends and relatives of both families present. After a short stay in Virginia, the newlyweds and their entourage of slaves headed west. General Clark was anxious to resume his duties as Superintendent of Indian Affairs in St. Louis, and to cover for his friend Governor Lewis—who was still nowhere to be found. (Note 3)

Note 1, Stephen Ambrose, *Undaunted Courage,* (New York, Simon and Schuster, 1996), Page 440.

Note 2, Ibid, Page 440.

Note 3, Jay H. Buckley, *William Clark-Indian Diplomat,* (Norman, OK, University of Oklahoma Press, 2008), Page 69.

CHAPTER 77

The Clarks of Louisville

When William Clark and his new bride arrived at his now "old Kentucky home" in Louisville, Kentucky, in the spring of 1808, no doubt many parties and balls were held in their honor. Brother Jonathan and his family was living at Trough Spring—a house designed by George Rogers Clark, and built under the supervision of William Clark in 1802—before he went west with Meriwether Lewis. (Note 1)

Although the house has been modified since the 19th century, it is the only other remaining structure from the original Clarks of Kentucky family—other than Locust Grove. Ironically, Trough Spring is a private home off of Dundee Road in the Highlands of Louisville, and is not open for tourism. It was to there that William sent letters and artifacts to Jonathan during his historic trip west with Meriwether Lewis. William and Julia also often stayed at Trough Spring with Jonathan, when going back and forth between St. Louis and the east.

William's Sister Lucy and her husband William Croghan (pronounced Crawn) had built Locust Grove in 1790, and was home to their now large family. With its second floor ballroom, Locust Grove was most likely the focal point of William and Julia Clark's wedding celebrations.

Except for George Rogers Clark, most of the rest of the Clark family was living at Mulberry Hill—the original Clark family home in Louisville. George Rogers Clark—the hero of the Revolutionary War in the west, was still living in his log cabin in the Indiana Territory overlooking the Ohio River—due to his financial problems stemming from the war. The old general, now fifty-six, was no doubt even more proud now of his seventeen year younger brother, and Williams many accomplishments.

Perhaps George Rogers Clark was now living vicariously through William's new acquisition—a wife that that George perhaps yearned for, but never got—the beautiful Spanish Princess Theresa de Leyba.

Perhaps in early May of 1808, there were horse races run at the Woodbourne Race Track (near present day St. Matthews but shut down in the early 1850's due to financial problems). The Clark families were always interested in horses. After all, the only transportation of the time was by water, by walking, by horseback, and by horse and carriage. (Note 2)

In any case, perhaps Julia said to her new husband, Billie why don't we stay here in Louisville. I love your family already. William's answer may have been—I hope for this also dear one, but my duties are in St. Louis for now.

Note 1, Historic plaque in front of Trough Spring.

Note 2, Historic plaque at site of track.

CHAPTER 78
The Clarks of St. Louis

After many sad farewells, now General William Clark and his bride Julia set off in two keelboats down the Ohio River on June 2, 1808. The boats were also loaded with their household furniture, an entourage of slaves, and of course York—William's loyal personal helper. General Clark had also brought larger gifts for the Indians this time—a one horse-power mill to grind grain, and blacksmith tools. The trip had also added the beautiful and accomplished and brilliant Miss Anderson—the daughter of William's sister Elizabeth. (Note 1)

Fortunately for William, his partner Meriwether Lewis had gotten his act together, and had arrived in St. Louis on March 8, 1808. Lewis had assumed his duties as governor of the Louisiana Territory, and had started a mission plan for the territory. (Note 2)

Even though communication was slow and primitive, Lewis had arranged for now Ensign Pryor—to meet his partner where the Ohio River meets the Mississippi and provide a military escort up the Mississippi River to St. Louis. After all, they had successfully done this before. Perhaps Meriwether Lewis was trying to make up for his disappearance during the period of the wedding, and the winter of 1808. (Note 3)

When the Clark family arrived in St. Louis, Meriwether Lewis led them to the house he had rented for them at a high cost of $250.00 per year. It was the best he could do. The house at Main and Spruce Streets in St. Louis had four rooms on the first floor, a second floor for the slaves, a detached kitchen, a garden, and a stable. Now the bad news—the house had only one bathroom—a smokehouse converted into an outhouse. This was certainly not what William Clark wanted for his new society bride from Virginia—or for his sheltered niece from Louisville. (Note 4)

Nevertheless, the Clark family soon adapted to the somewhat frontier life of St. Louis. The beautiful and brilliant Miss Anderson of Kentucky was soon the talk of the young men of the area. It is said that a town meeting was held to prevent any bloodshed from fighting over her. A lottery was held, and the winner would have the right to court Miss Anderson—the niece of William Clark. Thus, the Clarks of Kentucky and Virginia started to become the Clarks of St. Louis. (Note 5)

Note 1, Stephen Ambrose, *Undaunted Courage,* (New York, Simon and Schuster, 1996), Page 448.

Note 2, Ibid, Page 447.

Note 3, Ibid, Page 448.

Note 4, Ibid, Page 448.

Note 5, Ibid, Page 449.

CHAPTER 79
Lewis and Clark—Business and Pleasure in St. Louis

For the rest of the year of 1808 the two great men were very busy in St. Louis. Governor Lewis was trying to assume his new duties, but was more interested in making money in the fur trading business. To this end Lewis help to start the St. Louis Missouri River Fur Company. Among the partners were William Clark, their friends the Chouteau's, and other prominent St. Louis businessmen. Governor Lewis was most likely a silent partner—due to his concern about conflict of interest. The governor gave the new company exclusive trading rights up the Missouri River. (Note 1)

Brigadier General William Clark had an immediate major Indian problem—Big White was still in town. Ensign Nathaniel Pryor had tried to get the chief back to his Mandan people with a small force—sixteen hundred miles up the Missouri River. The problem was that the previously friendly Arikara Indians were now at war with the Mandans. They were not about to let an enemy chief get past their villages in the middle of the Missouri. Besides, the Arikaras were still mad about the death of their Chief Ankedouchera—who had gone to Washington before Big White, but died of natural causes in 1806 before returning. (Note 2)

Meanwhile, back at the new home of Julia and William Clark at Main and Spruce Streets in St. Louis, things were about to become more crowded—Julia was very pregnant. Soon Governor Lewis moved out—renting a room and office with their good friend Pierre

Chouteau. Lewis would still come to the Clarks house for most of his meals. (Note 3)

Note 1, Stephen Ambrose, *Undaunted Courage,* (New York, Simon and Schuster, 1996), Page 454.

Note 2, Ibid, Page 451.

Note 3, Ibid, Page 448.

CHAPTER 80

Enter Meriwether Lewis Clark

On January 10, 1809, Julia Hancock Clark delivered her first baby. They named him Meriwether Lewis Clark—in honor of William Clark's great partner and friend. Julia would later have two more boys: William Preston Clark—named in honor of William's friend who had introduced the couple, and George Rogers Hancock Clark—named in honor of William's famous brother, and Julia's father. (Note 1)

As much as Meriwether Lewis must have been elated by his great friend and partner naming his first born son in his honor, Lewis was not doing well as governor of the new territory. Lewis was a great military leader of men, but not a good politician. This soon led to his heavier drinking, and possibly some drug use.

In 1809 there was another big problem for Governor Lewis. James Madison was now President. His mentor Thomas Jefferson had retired to Monticello—to concentrate on founding The University of Virginia. At this point, the problems in the western territory were not a high priority for the new president. President Madison had a bigger problem to face in the east and south—the British were seizing American ships and impressing American sailors. Thus, with war looming with England, President Madison could not honor Governor Lewis' request for arms and men to help American traders go north to trade on the Missouri River—or to return one Indian chief home—as promised by the previous administration.

Nevertheless, Governor Lewis got enough men, weapons, and supplies to get Big White back to his Mandan people—in the summer of 1809. Still using his platinum credit card, Lewis ran up a very large bill of $7,000 to pay for the trip. He would set off in the fall of 1809 to go to Washington to justify his expenses. (Note 2)

Ironically, when Big White returned to his people, he was ridiculed. His truthful tales of what happened on the journey and in Washington D. C. were so astonishing to the Indians, that they thought he was a big liar. The poor man was guilty of only one thing—becoming Americanized, and doing exactly what President Jefferson had naively hoped that all Indians would do.

Big White had many other names, namely—Shahaka, Le Gros Blanc, Grand Blanc, Sheheke-Shote, White Coyote, and Bag of Lies. The last name was no doubt made up upon his return from the trip east. Great White was unfortunately killed by Sioux Indians in 1815. He should have stayed in St. Louis. (Note 3)

Note 1, Wikipedia, the free encyclopedia—William Clark (explorer).

Note 2, Stephen Ambrose, *Undaunted Courage,* (New York, Simon and Schuster, 1996), Page 461.

Note 3, Stephanie Ambrose Tubbs with Clay Straus Jenkinson, *The Lewis and Clark Companion,* (New York, Henry Holt and Company, LLC, 2003), Page 278.

CHAPTER 81

The Demise of Meriwether Lewis

As fall approached in St. Louis in 1809, Governor Lewis was becoming more at odds with secretary, Frederick Bates. Bates had been acting governor of the Louisiana Territory until Meriwether Lewis had been appointed governor by President Jefferson. Now, with a new administration in place in Washington, D. C., everything was changing.

Secretary Bates was resentful of Governor Lewis' aristocratic behavior and loose spending habits. He may have also started to report Lewis' possible conflict of interest in trying to profit from fur trading up the Missouri River—at the American taxpayer's expense. (Note 1)

Governor Lewis was starting to drink more, and borrow money from his friend General Clark—apparently due to his failed land speculation deals. As his problems mounted, Meriwether Lewis decided to head to Washington to justify his method of governing the Louisiana Territory, and the expenses he had incurred.

As Governor Lewis approached Washington in the fall of 1809, he apparently became more depressed—thinking about how to justify the $7,000.00 spent to get Chief Big White back to the Mandans. Lewis was perhaps also depressed when thinking of his failed love life—the beautiful Letitia Breckinridge had been recently married. Seeing his partner and best friend happily married, and with a new son, probably added to Meriwether Lewis' down moods. He also had no troops to lead, and his politics were a failure.

As Meriwether Lewis headed up the Naches Trace Trail toward Washington, he decided to stay overnight at a small inn some sixty miles south of Nashville, Tennessee—owned by a Mrs. Grinder. At some point during the early morning hours of October 11, 1809, the great man took his own life. What a waste of a young hero—Meriwether Lewis was only thirty-five years old. (Note 2)

William Clark was devastated when he confirmed the news of Meriwether Lewis' death on October 28th. At this point no one knew that the fallen hero's name would live on famously for a number of generations.

Note 1, Jay H. Buckley, *William Clark-Indian Diplomat,*(Norman, OK, University of Oklahoma Press, 2008), Page 81.

Note 2, Stephen Ambrose, *Undaunted Courage,* (New York, Simon and Schuster, 1996), Page 475.

CHAPTER 82
William Clark Continues his Career in St. Louis

Although he was still very sad about the loss of his great friend and partner Meriwether Lewis, William Clark continued to do a good job as Indian agent for the Louisiana Territory. He and Julia enjoyed a good life in St. Louis as they added to their family.

On June 16, 1813, William Clark was appointed by President Madison to be governor of the newly created Missouri Territory. The term was to be three years—with an ample salary of $2,000 per year. Governor Clark was also to continue to act as Indian agent for the Louisiana Territory. (Note 1)

As the war of 1812 with the British was heating up in the east and near New Orleans, people of the Missouri Territory were being harassed and killed by marauding Indians from up the Mississippi River—supported by their British trading partners. In a bold but unauthorized military move, Governor Clark decided to take the fight up river. He rounded up two gunboats, sixty regular soldiers, and one hundred militia troops. Clark and Major Zachary Taylor left St. Louis on May 1, 1814. This time William Clark's main keelboat (which he named the *Governor Clark*) had thirty-two oars and fourteen swivel cannons. As a comparison the Corps of Discovery's keelboat had only one swivel cannon and twenty-two oars. (Note 2)

The well armed armada soon captured the area of Prairie du Chen, over six hundred miles upstream from St. Louis—near present day Dubuque, Iowa. After defeating the British and Indians there, Governor

Clark started to build a fort where the Wisconsin and Missouri Rivers converge. He named it Fort Shelby, in honor of Kentucky's first governor—Isaac Shelby.

After leaving sixty-five men to build the fort and his gunboat, the *Governor Clark* with its eighty man crew, Governor Clark returned to St. Louis. He was again treated as a hero, and called "the shield of the territory". (Note 3)

Unfortunately for William Clark, his victory was short-lived, similar to his brother George's taking the fort at Vincennes the first time during the Revolution. Like British Governor Hamilton (a. k. a. "The Hair Buyer") taking a large force of British troops and Indians to recapture Vincennes, a British Captain McKay had a force of six hundred British troops and Indians. In a surprise attack, the British cut the lines of the *Governor Clark* gunboat and sent it harmlessly down the Mississippi. They soon overwhelmed the small American force in the unfinished fort. Captain McKay even renamed the fort after himself. (Note 3)

Although Governor Clark would get no reinforcements from the American War Department to help retake Prairie du Chen, he would eventually get his revenge—just as brother George did in retaking the fort at Vincennes. In William's case, he did at least have his military expenses eventually paid—which could have bankrupted him, just as it did George Rogers Clark. Just as in the Revolutionary War, the western part of the country was not as important to defend in the War of 1812.

Note 1, Jay H. Buckley, *William Clark-Indian Diplomat,* (Norman, OK, University of Oklahoma Press, 2008), Page 89.
Note 2, Ibid, Page 105.
Note 3, Ibid, Page 106.

CHAPTER 83

St. Louis and the Missouri Territory Dodge the Bullet

While Governor William Clark and his small military force was having trouble with the British and Indians north of St. Louis, the fledgling country was about to have a larger British problem looming near New Orleans. British General Edward Packenham had helped to defeat Napoleon at a number of battles in 1813-1814. He came to America with 9,000 veteran troops in twenty-five British ships of the line. Many were probably forcibly manned by impressed American sailors, the initial cause of the War of 1812. (Note 1)

General Packenham's plan was grandiose and simple. First he would take New Orleans. Then he would sail his warships up the Mississippi River, establish forts along the way, and meet up with their British forces—and their Indian allies—coming south from Canada. Thus, for America losing New Orleans and control of he Mississippi River, would also mean losing the Louisiana Purchase. This would nullify the value of Lewis and Clark's expedition, and cost America $15,000,000 precious dollars. The British might also try to take back the rest of the America—from west to east—and possibly use St. Louis as their new capitol. (Note 2)

Governor William Clark with his limited funds and his militia, had already found it impossible to defend his Missouri Territory from the British and their Indian allies. Even the gallant Major Zachary Taylor with 350 men and eight gunboats could not get past a large force of Canadians and four hundred Indians to retake Prairie du Chen.

Fortunately for America, President Madison had the foresight to promote Andrew Jackson to General, and send him to New Orleans to stop the new British invasion. Jackson had fought in two successful battles against Indians, but had never faced a veteran British army.

On December 2, 1814, Andrew Jackson took his militia and a few regulars (about 800 total) into New Orleans and declared martial law. He then drafted men of all nationalities and colors to defend the city. He even had civilians building earthworks to use as shields from British artillery and gunfire. (Note 3)

As preparations continued, General Jackson assembled a rag-tag army of almost 4,000 men by late December of 1814. Although many of the men were not fond of America's occupation of New Orleans, they had an intense dislike of the British. Jackson even recruited Jean Lafitte the pirate to fight for America—his men were obviously very handy when using cannons.

On December 26, 1812, General Packenham started to move his army of 10,000 men toward the American lines. After a few minor skirmishes, the real battle started on New Years Day of 1815. At a distance of three hundred yards, the two sides exchanged cannon fire—Jackson's thirteen to Packenham's fourteen. The British fired rapidly, but failed to adjust the elevation of their cannons—causing most of their shells to go harmlessly over the American breastworks. The Americans fired slowly but accurately, soon knocking all of the British cannons out of commission—while losing only two. (Note 4)

Minor firing continued until the morning of January 8, 1815, when General Packenham sent the main part of his army to within 400 yards of the American lines. With their scarlet red uniforms, and white crossed straps, they continued marching—with bayonets fixed—to rout the rag-tag American army. After all, they had defeated the best armies in Europe this way. When the British drew within 100 yards, General Jackson gave the order to fire at will—by using a fourteen year old free black youth named Noble to beat his drum—as a pre-arranged signal.

The Kentucky and Tennessee sharpshooters wreaked havoc on the advancing British soldiers. After many casualties, the British army started to retreat. General Packenham rallied his troops and led them forward again. The British were again met with a wall of American rifle fire. General Packenham and another general were both killed—causing another retreat. A third general tried to rally the troops again and was also killed. (Note 5)

The battle was over within a half-hour, with the British suffering almost 2,000 casualties. The Americans lost fewer than fifty-five men.

General Packenham's body was taken to a ship by the retreating British—and put into an empty rum barrel to be returned to England. His glorious plan of conquest had failed in the worst way. (Note 6)

Ironically, The Treaty of Ghent had been signed on December 24, 1814, bringing peace to both sides. Thus, The Battle of New Orleans was fought two weeks after the War of 1812 was officially over. The battle did serve a good purpose, however, by showing that The United States of America was here to stay—and a force with which to be reckoned.

In the Missouri Territory, Governor Clark and his St. Louis associates were thrilled to know that their British problem was basically over. They would, however, still face many more years of Indian problems.

Note 1, Stephen E. Ambrose, *To America,* (New York, Simon and Schuster, 2002), Page 16.

Note 2, Ibid, Page 16.

Note 3, Ibid, Page 19.

Note 4, Ibid, Page 21.

Note 5, Ibid, Page 23.

Note 6, Ibid, Page 24.

CHAPTER 84

Governor Clark Helps to Create the State of Missouri

With the British problem now minimized, William Clark started to concentrate his energy on creating the state of Missouri—just as brother George had done in Kentucky. As governor of the territory and chief Indian agent he was in a great position to do so.

Working with surveyors to help create boundaries, and many Indian agents under his supervision, Governor Clark used his diplomatic skills to move many Indians out of Missouri. He got the Osage, the Shawnee, and many other tribes to move west and north of Missouri for very little compensation for their land.

With many more white settlers moving in, and the Indians moving out, Missouri was poised to become a state by 1820. The obvious choice to become governor of the new state would be the chief architect of statehood, and governor of the territory—William Clark, formally of Kentucky.

Unfortunately for William Clark, a number of events and some negative campaigning by supporters of his opponent would hurt Clark's chances. Although we tend to think of negative advertising in a political race as a new trend, it was also used in 1820. Alexander McNair was also a strong candidate—and a friend of Clark's. McNair did a good job of running the United States Land Office in St. Louis. McNair even told Clark that he would not have run if he knew that Clark was going to run. Some of McNair's supporters did promote negative things about William Clark—saying that he was too lenient with the Indians, and had not protected new settlers against attacks. They even claimed that Clark had an Indian wife and Indian children. Does that sound similar to the negative television political commercials of today? (Note 1)

In fact, Sacagawea and her husband Charbonneau, and their children Jean Babtiste (Pomp) and Lizette did visit the Clarks in St. Louis in 1810—returning north in 1812. The children boarded with the Clarks and were tutored there. They were probably tutored by Julia Clark, with Meriwether Lewis Clark (now being called Lewis) present also—he was only four years younger than Pomp. Jean Baptiste/Pomp would have a long and colorful life in Europe and the American west. Details are sketchy about the history of the rest of the Charbonneau family. (Note 2)

Although the negative press may have had some effect on William Clark's run for governor of Missouri, the main negative factor was his lack of campaigning—due to his personal problems. Prior to 1820, Julia Clark had become ill, and had been sent home to Virginia to receive better care and get well. Upon receiving word that her condition was not improving, William Clark left St. Louis on March 23, 1820—just after announcing his intention to run for governor of Missouri—and taking his last oath as governor of the Missouri Territory. (Note 3)

While McNair was campaigning for governor of Missouri, William Clark was in Virginia tending to his sick wife. His only campaigning was through his written statements, and help from his nephew John O'Fallon—the son of his sister Fanny. O'Fallon did get a number of articles published stressing William Clark's service to America and the Missouri Territory. (Note 4)

Unfortunately for William Clark, his lovely Julia died on June 27, 1820—probably of cancer. She was only twenty-eight years old. William was now a widower with five young children to raise: Meriwether Lewis—age eleven; William Preston—age eight; Mary Margaret—age six; George Rogers Hancock—age four, and John Julius—age two. Mary Margaret had gone to live in Kentucky with Julia's sister Caroline, and unfortunately died in 1821 at age seven. John Julius stayed in Virginia with his grandparents—due to a physical disability. (Note 5)

As William Clark and his three sons sadly made their way back to St. Louis, they visited their family in Kentucky. William was still very sad about the passing of his hero and mentor brother on February 13, 1818. No doubt prayers were said over his grave at Locust Grove.

When William and the boys finally arrived in St. Louis, the election for the first governor of the new state was about to be held. There was little time for Clark to campaign, and he was probably not in a mood to do so anyway. More bad news—on September 20, 1820, William Clark loses the election for governor of Missouri to his friend Alexander McNair—6,576 votes to 2,556 votes. The Clarks of Kentucky were down for now, but they would live to rise again. (Note 6)

Note 1, Jay H. Buckley, *William Clark-Indian Agent,* (Norman, OK, University of Oklahoma Press, 2008), Page 138.

Note 2, Ibid, Page 214.

Note 3, Ibid, Page 139.

Note 4, Ibid, Page 137.

Note 5, Ibid, Page 137.

Note 6, Ibid, Page 140.

CHAPTER 85
Citizen Clark Makes a Comeback

In late September of 1820, William Clark was just another plain American citizen. He had resigned his post of governor of the Missouri Territory in March of 1820 to run for governor of the new state of Missouri—which he had greatly helped to create. He had lost the election for governor on September 20, 1820.

Now at age fifty, William Clark had already earned many titles: Ensign and Lieutenant of the Kentucky militia; Captain of the Chosen Rifle Company of elite riflemen-sharpshooters in the U. S, Army; Co-captain (but only Lieutenant in actual pay scale) during the Lewis and Clark expedition; Brigadier General of Indian Affairs for the Louisiana Territory; and then Governor of the Missouri Territory.

William Clark was no doubt somewhat depressed at this point in time. Here he was in St. Louis at age fifty with no wife, no job, no title, no supporting family nearby, and three young sons to raise. The obvious solution was to return to his Kentucky and Virginia roots. Perhaps Lewis the oldest son—now at age eleven—said: dad, why don't we return to your old Kentucky home. (Note 1)

In any case, William and the three boys soon headed to Kentucky for support and encouragement with his family. After visiting with his daughter Mary Margaret in Louisville, and leaving the boys with relatives, William Clark headed to southern Virginia to visit his in-laws, and his other son John Julius.

While William was in Virginia, he again met up with Harriet Kennerly Radford, who was Julia's first cousin. As the Clark lore states, she was the other girl that William Clark helped to cross a creek when their horse acted up while they were riding double—many years before (Note 2)

Perhaps the relationship between William and Harriet was at first more of a merger than a love affair. Harriet was a widow with three small children, and William was a widower with three small children. She needed a husband to take care of she and her children, and he needed a wife to take care of his three boys.

In any case, William Clark at age fifty, and Harriet Kennerly Radford at age thirty-one were married in St. Louis on October28, 1821. Although from sketches by Kerry D. Sopher, Julia appears to be prettier than Harriet, she did a good job to help raise the six children. She also became a popular hostess while entertaining William's friends and business associates in St. Louis. (Note 3)

William Clark's lack of a job would also soon end. On May 6, 1822, Congress had created a new post: Superintendant of Indian Affairs at St. Louis—at a good salary of $1,500.00 per year. There was only one person in America who would qualify to supervise several hundred thousand Indians—William Clark. Thus, President James Monroe soon appointed William Clark to this position. William Clark had made a complete comeback. He would continue to do a masterful job as an Indian diplomat. The Clark legend of service and honor to America would continue. Meriwether Lewis Clark (Lewis) would soon start to add his part to the family legend. (Note 4)

Note 1, Jay H. Buckley, *William Clark-Indian Diplomat,* (Norman, OK, University of Oklahoma Press, 2008), Page 145.

Note 2, Ibid, Page 251.

Note 3, Ibid, Page 146.

Note 4, Ibid, Page 146.

CHAPTER 86
William Clark—Masterful Indian Agent

As William Clark settled into his job as Superintendant of Indian Affairs at St. Louis, he was dealing with Indians for his third President. First there was Thomas Jefferson, then James Madison, and now James Monroe. Through the 1830's he would serve two more Presidents—John Quincy Adams, and Andrew Jackson. In those early days of America, it was a credit to his skill as a diplomat that he could deal with the problems of relocating 100,000 Indians, while juggling orders from five very different Presidents. While Thomas Jefferson Wanted to be a father figure to the Indians and Americanize them, Andrew Jackson wanted Superintendant Clark to move the Indians west—or exterminate them. The philosophies of the other Presidents were somewhere in between the two extremes. (Note 1)

With the war of 1812 over, the new state of Missouri was attracting more white settlers. With more American military troops available, the Indians were becoming greatly outnumbered. Thus, in late August of 1825, William Clark called for a major council with many Indian tribes. It was held at Prairie du Chen—a major crossroads on the Mississippi River. We may recall the big, but short lived victory there for territorial Governor Clark of ten years before.

This time the now Superintendant Clark had a diplomatic victory. After two weeks of negotiating, most of the tribes agreed to move to the millions of acres west of the Missouri River—in present day Kansas and Oklahoma. These treaties would go far toward relocating many Indians west. Many Indians that were being removed were the remnants from the northeast and southeast tribes. (Note 2)

The cost to America was fairly cheap—amounting to $.75 per acre—except when a tribe did not keep their treaty. This would cause a war in 1832, when Chief Blackhawk of the Sauk tribe decided that he did not like the Americans' deal.

Blackhawk had violated the 1825 treaty of Prairie du Chen, by leaving most of his people at Rock River. This location is where Rock River meets the Mississippi (near present day Davenport, Iowa on the west side, and Rock Island, Illinois on the east side). After a number of moves back and forth across the Mississippi, the Black Hawk tribe, the Sauk, and his ally tribe of Fox Indians reoccupied their land at Rock River in Western Illinois. The governor of Illinois then sent out the militia to eliminate the problem. General Henry Atkinson sent Federal troops from St. Louis to help the Illinois forces.

A recently arrived second lieutenant in the 6th U. S. Infantry was assigned to fight in the Black Hawk War—his name was Meriwether Lewis Clark (Lewis). This would be his first combat since graduating from the new United States Military Academy in 1830. Superintendant William Clark could not go fight, and was no doubt sad to see his first born son go to war. It probably reminded him of his battles with Indians—The battle of Fallen Timbers in particular—and how big brother George and the Clark family worried about his safety. (Note 3)

In any case, Lewis performed his duties well as an officer and a mapmaker—just as dad had done in the past. The combined American armies chased Black Hawk and his followers across parts of Illinois and Wisconsin. Most of Black Hawk's people were killed along the banks of the Mississippi River. Most of those who made it across the Mississippi were killed by their enemies—the Sioux Indians. Chief Black Hawk was captured by a party of Winebago Indians and turned over to the Americans at Prairie du Chen. (Note 4)

Black Hawk was still a proud chief. He stated that he had just tried to do what was best for his people. He was taken to the Jefferson Barracks in St. Louis. Black Hawk and two of his sub-chiefs were held there, and then sent to Washington to meet President Andrew Jackson. Jackson then planned to have them imprisoned at Fort Monroe in Virginia.

Here again, Superintendant William Clark came to the rescue. He wrote to the Commissioner of Indian Affairs in Washington, asking for a pardon for the three chiefs. His argument was two-fold: first, the Indians had seen the might of the American armies; and second it would further the relations with other chiefs and tribes who had abided by their treaties.

Clark's idea was approved, and the three chiefs were released. In another brilliant suggestion, Superintendant Clark asked that the chiefs be given a tour of Baltimore, Philadelphia, and New York—to show them more of the might of America. This may have helped, since there were no more problems with Indians moving from the east to the west of the Missouri River. Even Black Hawk became reformed, and stated that the tomahawk is buried forever, and that the white man would always be welcome in his village as a brother. He died of natural causes in his lodge along the Iowa River in 1838. Ironically, William Clark—the great Indian diplomat—also died in 1838—one month later. (Note 5)

Note 1, Jay H. Buckley, *William Clark-Indian Diplomat,* (Norman, OK, University of Oklahoma Press, 2008), Pages 193-195.
Note 2, Ibid, Pages 172-174.
Note 4, Ibid, Pages209-210.
Note 5, Ibid, Page 211.
Note 3, Wikipedia, Meriwether Lewis Clark, Sr.

CHAPTER 87
Meriwether Lewis Clark (Lewis) Starts to Grow Up

As Meriwether Lewis Clark grew up in St. Louis, he also enjoyed a good social life—probably due to the fame of his father. But what should his friends call him? Meriwether is an honorable name, but too long. If shortened to Meri, it sounds feminine. Thus, his most commonly used name became his middle name—Lewis.

As Lewis grew up, he was home-schooled by his mother Julia, and step-mother Harriet. Despite his lack of a formal education, Lewis was appointed to the fairly new United States Military Academy in 1826. It was no doubt dad's influence that got Lewis the appointment. He probably said—don't worry dad, I wont let you down. In any case, he graduated in four years—finishing 23rd out of 42 cadets. His brilliant mind would be shown in a number of ways in the future. (Note 1)

The founding of The United States Military Academy at West Point, New York had been led by President Jefferson in 1804—and supported by Secretary of War Dearborn. Their motives were to develop good officers for the American army, and partially to influence French businessmen in the new Louisiana Territory to send their sons to West Point. This in turn would hopefully help to increase their loyalty to the new nation. (Note 2)

The other clever thing that Jefferson an Dearborn did was to make it a condition that a graduate of West Point must serve four years of military service for his country. After all, each cadet had been given a free four year technical college education. This rule is still in force in modern day America. The U. S. Naval Academy was soon founded on the same principles—and later the Coast Guard and Air Force Academies.

Meriwether Lewis Clark, not wanting to make a career of the army, resigned his commission in 1833—as soon as his four years were up. He was anxious to pursue a career in architecture.

After returning home to St. Louis, Lewis soon went to Louisville, Kentucky to visit relatives. While there, Lewis met Abigail Prather Churchill. Abigail was from one of the first families of Kentucky. The Churchills had moved to Louisville in 1787, and bought three hundred acres of land in a rural area, south of the city. The Clarks and the Churchills were almost neighbors—with Mulberry Hill and Trough Spring being only a mile or two from the Churchill land.

In any case, Lewis at age twenty-three, courted and won the hand of sixteen year old Abigail Prather Churchill. They were married on January 9, 1834, in St. Louis, where Lewis was starting to build a successful career as a designer-architect. He contributed a lot to the early architecture of St. Louis. He even designed the St. Vincent de Paul Roman Catholic Church. In 1886 Lewis was elected to the Missouri General Assembly. (Note 3)

As Lewis' career and reputation grew, his famous father was in failing health. Lewis, at age twenty-nine would soon become the next head of the famous Clark family.

Note 1, Meriwether Lewis Clark, Sr.—Wikipedia, the free encyclopedia

Note 2, Stephen Ambrose, *Undaunted Courage,* (New York, Simon and Schuster, 1996), Page 136.

Note 3, Meriwether Lewis Clark, Sr.—Wikipedia, the free encyclopedia

CHAPTER 88
The Great William Clark Passes On

As William Clark headed into his sixties, his health started to fail. He was still active as a great Indian agent and diplomat, but his territorial jurisdictions were decreased by Congress. There were now four districts of Indian affairs—but Clark's was still the largest.

In the fall of 1831 (or by one account December 25), William's second wife Harriet passed away—this time only one child was still at home. Lewis at age twenty-two was now serving the army, but still possibly being somewhat spoiled by his loving father. William Preston Clark, at age twenty was enrolled at the University of Virginia (and later attended Harvard Law School). George Rogers Hancock Clark was attending Augusta College in Kentucky. Jefferson Kearney Clark, Harriet and William's only living child was the only one left at home for William to care for. (Note 1)

William Clark now became more of an ambassador to entertain artists, authors, and dignitaries who wanted to go west into Indian country. He would also give the men letters of introduction to the various friendly chiefs. For example, William Clark met the famous author Washington Irving, our French hero from the Revolution, the Marquis de Lafayette, and a German nobleman named Prince Paul. The prince would later reciprocate by taking Sacagawea's son Jean Baptiste Charbonneau—or Pomp as Clark called him—to Germany for a five year visit and education. (Note 2)

Governor Clark also tried to help the Indians by sending doctors to the various reservations—to inoculate them against smallpox. Although a few thousand Indians did receive the smallpox vaccine, many more thousands were killed by not wanting to take the shot. For example, the Mandan and Arikara Indians—great friends of the Lewis and Clark expedition—were decimated by smallpox. This, of course, upset William Clark greatly.

At age sixty-six Governor Clark negotiated his last treaty with the Indians. It was his thirty-seventh treaty, called the Platte Purchase—which added land to the state of Missouri. (Note 3)

As William Clark's health continued to decline, he would spend more time at son Lewis' house. He passed away there on September 1, 1838—at age sixty-eight. Meriwether Lewis Clark at age twenty-nine, and his twenty-one year old wife Abigail Prather Churchill Clark were now in charge of the family. At least at this point, all of William Clark's children were old enough to be on their own.

William Clark had had been a St. Louis icon for three decades, and was revered by most people in Missouri and Kentucky. His funeral was the largest was the largest in St. Louis at the time, as thousands of people lined up along the route from Lewis' home to William Clark's burial site at Bellefontaine Cemetery. (Note 4)

Although other Clarks of Kentucky were famous before and after William, he was probably the most famous Clark—a great soldier, a great explorer, a great statesman, and a great patriot.

Note 1, Jay H. Buckley, *William Clark-Indian Diplomat,* (Norman, OK, University of Oklahoma Press, 2008), Page 225.

Note 2, Ibid, Page 214.

Note 3, Ibid, Page 227.

Note 4, Ibid, Page 232.

Chapter 89

Lewis Fights in the Mexican War

After dad William passed away in 1838, Lewis and wife Abby enjoyed the good life in St. Louis as the next generation of the famous Clark family. They would soon add to the population of St. Louis, with William Hancock Clark, Samuel Churchill Clark, and Meriwether Lewis Clark, Jr.—the latter born on January 26, 1846. (Note 1)

In 1845 Texas became an American state—with the southern border being in dispute with Mexico. While the Americans claimed the Rio Grande River as the border, The Mexicans claimed that it was the Nueces River—about one hundred fifty miles north. President James Polk had sent Zachary Taylor—now a general—to protect the Rio Grande Border. When a force of two thousand Mexican cavalry attacked an American patrol of seventy, and killed sixteen U. S. soldiers, America declared war on Mexico—on May 13, 1846. (Note 2)

Like his famous uncle George, and his famous father William, Lewis also felt that it was again his duty to serve his country. He enlisted as a major in the Missouri volunteers, and served as a commander of an artillery battalion. Perhaps he was recruited by his Kentucky families' neighbor—Zachary Taylor—with whom Lewis had seen service in the Black Hawk War, and with whom father William had fought Indians.

Thus, as Lewis was off to war, he left Abby with four young children to raise—not knowing if, or when he would be back. Abby at age twenty-nine, with Lewis' going business, could afford help with the children. She would need help, since her youngest—Meriwether Lewis Clark, Jr. was less than a year old.

Most of the war was fought below the Rio Grande River in Mexican territory. Lewis fought in one of the minor battles under Colonel Alexander Doniphan on February 28, 1847—where they easily took Chihuahua City in northern Mexico. Many of the battles were hard-fought and bloody, with the Americans even taking Mexico City. General Zachary Taylor became famous during the war with his daring exploits. He also defeated the famous Mexican General Antonio Lopez de Santa Ana at the battle of Buena Vista, while being outnumbered four to one. He probably rallied the troops by saying—remember the Alamo! (Note 3)

The Mexican-American War ended with 16,000 Mexican casualties, and over 13,000 American casualties. Before the war, President James Polk had offered Mexico over thirty million American dollars for the disputed Rio Grande territory, and all of the Mexican territory north and west to the Pacific Ocean. With the Mexican government in disarray as usual, the offer was turned down. Ironically after the war, when the Mexicans had no choice, they agreed that the Rio Grande would be the border between Mexico and The United States.

Mexico also ceded the present day states of California, Nevada, Utah, New Mexico, most of Arizona and Colorado, and parts of Texas, Oklahoma, Kansas, and Wyoming. For this America paid Mexico $18,250,000 as part of the Treaty of Guadalupe Hidalgo—signed on February 2, 1848. The treaty also agreed for the American government to assume $3,250,000 owed by the Mexican government to U. S. citizens. The money Mexico received was less than half that President Polk had offered before the war. (Note 4)

President James K. Polk does not get enough credit for being a nation builder. Polk helped to add another one-third of the continent to America, just as President Jefferson had done with the Louisiana Purchase. It is hard to believe that two-thirds of the United States was bought for less than forty million dollars—not billions or trillions—terms we throw around in government spending in modern times.

Thus, Meriwether Lewis Clark, by fighting in the Mexican War, was a small part in the final major expansion in America.

Note 1, Meriwether Lewis Clark, Jr.—Wikipedia, the free encyclopedia. Pg 1
Note 2, Mexican-American War—Wikipedia, the free encyclopedia, Page 5.
Note 3, Zachary Taylor—Wikipedia, the free encyclopedia, Page 3.
Note 4, Mexican-American War, Wikipedia, the free encyclopedia, Pages 12-13.

CHAPTER 90

Life in St. Louis in Between Wars

With the Mexican War over in February of 1848, Lewis returned to St. Louis to resume his architectural and civil engineering career. He was soon appointed as the Federal Surveyor General for Missouri and Illinois.

Abby, now at age thirty-one, was no doubt glad to have Lewis home to help to raise their four children. Meriwether Lewis Clark, Jr. was in his "terrible twos", and probably starting to show signs of a temper—similar to his namesake. Abby would be kept busy while bearing Lewis three more sons: John O'Fallon Clark in 1850, George Rogers Clark (II) in 1851, and Charles Jefferson Clark in 1852. Unfortunately she would die soon after giving birth on January 14, 1852. This, of course, was not uncommon in the early days of medical technology—Abby was only two months from her thirty-sixth birthday. (Note 1)

Lewis was devastated by her loss, and now found himself in the same situation as father William had been—a widowed father with young children to raise. In Lewis' case, his youngest was just born, and his oldest—William Hancock Clark was thirteen.

What to do? Like father William, Lewis had many friends and associates in St. Louis, but no close relatives. Like William, Lewis would ask for help from relatives in Louisville, Kentucky. This time the children were taken in by Abby's relatives—the Churchill's of Kentucky—with many Clark relatives nearby to help. Fortunately, the children's aunt and her two bachelor sons, John and Henry Churchill had the means to raise—and probably spoil Abby's children. (Note 2)

As much as Lewis would have preferred to be in Louisville with his children, his duties were in Missouri—as a successful architect and civil engineer. Where did this great technical mind come from? It was apparently a trait inherited from the first Clarks of Kentucky—Ann Rogers Clark and John Clark—his grandparents. Uncle George Rogers Clark was not only a brilliant military technical genius, but was working on a method to drive boats up river—using the recently invented steam engine. He was also working on plans for a canal to be used to circumvent the falls of the Ohio. He, of course, did design a number of forts—for the protection of Louisville and Kentucky. Unfortunately for George, his tangled Revolutionary War monetary problems kept him from pursuing any of his technical ideas. (Note 3)

William Clark also had a very technically oriented mind. His brilliant mapmaking skills during the Lewis and Clark expedition were invaluable to future American explorers. He also used his technical mind to make improvements to the Corps of Discovery keelboat.

Lewis was fortunate to be the first in the Clark family to get a formal education—and use it to great advantage. Just as Lewis was getting his career in high gear after the loss of his wife Abby, and getting his children settled in Kentucky, another war was brewing—this time between Americans.

Note 1, Meriwether Lewis Clark, Sr.—Wikipedia, the free encyclopedia, Pg 1
Note 2, Ibid, Page 1.
Note 3, Britannica Concise Encyclopedia: George Rogers Clark, Page 4.

CHAPTER 91
Lewis Reluctantly Goes to War Again

When Fort Sumpter in Charleston, South Carolina was fired on, April 12, 1861, The American Civil War started. South Carolina had been the first state to secede from The United States on December 20, 1860. Border States like Maryland, Kentucky, and Missouri were now greatly divided on the issue of secession.

With the war started, all states—weather north, south, or neutral—started to organize their armies. Governor Claiborne F. Jackson of Missouri—a pro-secessionist—appointed Meriwether Lewis Clark (Lewis), to organize the Ninth District of Missouri—knowing that Lewis was also strongly pro-secessionist. Lewis was now a brigadier general in the Ninth Division of the Missouri State Guard. Although the state of Missouri was evenly divided over secession, St. Louis was strongly pro-union. Thus, Lewis would have trouble getting recruits, and the unit was never formally organized. Lewis resigned his commission in November of 1861. (Note 1)

Although Lewis was not involved, the second skirmish of the Civil War happened when President Lincoln sent Federal troops to St. Louis, fearing that Missouri Governor Jackson would have his troops take over the Federal Arsenal there (after all, it had happened at Harpers Ferry in 1859), arm his men, and secede from the Union. A fiery Union Captain Nathaniel Lyon, while dispersing the governor's men near the arsenal, killed twenty civilians in the process. Although Lyon was killed in a small battle soon after, and although Missouri never did secede, bitter feelings remained on both sides for the rest of the war. (Note 2)

These events no doubt influenced Lewis to cut his ties with Missouri and St. Louis, and go to defend his Virginia roots. After all, his wife had passed away, and his children were in Kentucky. Lewis soon went east, and accepted a commission of major of artillery in the Confederate Army. After all, who to better serve for, than his friend and classmate from the U. S. Military Academy—General Robert E. Lee. (Note 3)

Lewis was soon promoted to Colonel of Artillery under General Braxton Bragg. He commanded Bragg's artillery at the battle of Stone's River near Murfreesboro, Tennessee in early January of 1863. He was lucky not to be killed, since the Confederate Army lost nearly 12,000 men, and the Union Army lost over 13,000 men. When Union reinforcements arrived, the Rebels were forced to retire. Lewis was then put in charge of the Ordnance Department in the defense of the South's capitol of Richmond, Virginia.

In November of 1864, Lewis was promoted to brigadier general, and assumed command of an infantry brigade, serving directly under his friend Robert E. Lee—in the Army of Northern Virginia. General Lee's valiant but now ill-supplied, and greatly outnumbered army headed west from Richmond which had fallen—in early April of 1865. On April 6th, at the battle of Sayler's Creek, near Amelia Courthouse, Lee lost half of his remaining army to General Sheridan—with six thousand Rebel soldiers captured. Brigadier General Meriwether Lewis Clark, Sr. was one of the men captured. Three days later General Lee, realizing that there was now no chance to win the war, surrendered to General Grant in the McLean house at Appomattox Courthouse. Lewis was soon released, being fortunate to make it through the war unharmed, and to be a prisoner of war for only a short time. (Note 4)

What did Lewis say to himself after being freed? Perhaps he said, I am now fifty-six years old and through with military service. I have very few ties to St. Louis, and my children are in Kentucky. My youngest son is thirteen, and Junior is now nineteen. I wonder what he is up to. I can restart my architectural and engineering careers in Kentucky—and I might get married again. I still miss my dear Abby very much, but I have been a widower for thirteen years.

Note 1, Meriwether Lewis Clark, Sr.-Wikipedia, the free encyclopedia, Pg 2.

Note 2, Richard M. Ketchum, *The Civil War,* (New York, NY, American Heritage Publishing Company, Incorporated, 1960), Page 63.

Note 3, Meriwether Lewis Clark, Sr.-Wikipedia, the free encyclopedia, Pg 2.

Note 4, Ibid, Page 2.

CHAPTER 92

Life in Louisville Kentucky—
After the Civil War

When Meriwether Louis Clark, Sr. (Lewis) arrived in Louisville in 1865, he was no doubt thrilled to be reunited with his children and other relatives. The Churchill's were probably glad to have Lewis nearby to help share the responsibilities of raising his and Abby's seven children.

Louisville had not been devastated like many other southern cities, due to being a neutral border state. The economy had, however, had suffered somewhat by being occupied under martial law by Northern troops. Also, many families were still split over their views of the war.

After the war, the economy and most social relations started to get better. Lewis, the latest famous Clark of Kentucky wasted no time getting into Louisville society. After all, he was a well known architect, civil engineer, a brigadier general, and a veteran of three wars. And, of course, everyone knew of his famous father William Clark, and his famous uncle George Rogers Clark. Julia Davidson must have been impressed with Lewis—they were married on December 30, 1865. (Note 1)

With Meriwether Lewis Clark, Sr., and Meriwether Lewis Clark, Jr. now in the same town again as adults, what do we call Junior? The family apparently settled on the name of "Lutie". Being an ambitious young man of nineteen when father Lewis arrived, Lutie was a better name than Junior or Meriwether—despite the famous and noble connection.

With Lewis now in Louisville, the subject of horses no doubt came up during family get-togethers. After all, horses were a great part of Lewis' uncle George Rogers Clark's and his father William Clark's life—using them to explore, or fight wars, or just for transportation. Lewis, at one time had twenty-five horses in St. Louis—with most of them named. Names such as Bolivar, Saladin, Palestine, Troubadour, and Hector. He also had some horses with common names such as Sally, Tom, Old Joe, and Charley. Brothers John and Henry Churchill owned a number of horses—which they often raced through makeshift tracks in Louisville, or through the streets of Lexington. (Note 1)

As the Civil War disrupted the plantation system, racing fell on hard times. The Woodlawn Association Track in Louisville (near present day Hubbards Lane and Westport Road) closed in 1870—due to financial problems. Also, base ball (two words in 1860) had become popular in Louisville. The Louisville Grays became a famous professional team—until it was found out that some team members had been paid to lose games by professional gamblers. (Note 2)

Still, it can be seen how young Lutie might have developed some interest in horses. He was constantly being involved with horse talk from all of his Louisville relatives. Lutie's uncles, John and Henry Churchill continued their interest in thoroughbred horses and racing—despite its having fallen on hard times. Lutie's father Lewis would soon move to Frankfort, Kentucky to resume his architectural career. He would eventually design some buildings for the state capitol there. (Note 3)

Note 1, James J. Holmberg, *The Clark Family and the Kentucky Derby,* (Louisville, Ky., The Filson Hist. Soc., Newsmag., Vol. 4, No. 1), Pages 1-2.

Note 2, George H. Yater, *Two Hundred Years at the Falls of the Ohio,* Louisville, Ky., The Heritage Corp., 1979), Page 112.

Note 3, Meriwether Lewis Clark, Sr.-Wikipedia, the free encyclopedia, Pg 2

CHAPTER 93

Lutie Goes to Europe—to Study Thoroughbred Racing

At this point in 1870 there were only six thoroughbred tracks in America—including the Kentucky Association track in Lexington. They were all barely surviving at this point. The Clark family already had a three generation love affair with horses—many of them thoroughbreds. Thus, John and Henry Churchill, and some other breeders of Kentucky, in 1872 decided to send Lutie—now known as Colonel M. Lewis Clark—to study the thriving English and French racing industries. Lutie, now at age twenty-seven and newly married, was anxious to fulfill his assignment.

Upon arriving in England, Colonel Clark immediately got heavily involved with English racing. He was very impressed with the Epsom (English) Derby and The Epsom Oaks—both races run at a mile and one half for three-year-olds. The Derby being open to colts, geldings, and fillies, while the Oaks was for fillies only. Lutie also liked a race at two miles called the St. Leger—named for a Colonel St. Leger. Races in those days were usually long—with some races being run at three or four miles—and often the best of three heats. (Note 1)

The Epsom or (English) Derby is run at the Epsom Downs Course, and named for the estate "Epsom"—owned by the 12th Earl of Derby. The Darby—as the English call it—was first run in 1780. At first the pioneers of the thoroughbred industry in England could not decide on a name for this new race. Since Lord Derby and Sir Charles Bunbury had been the main contributors to initiate England's biggest race, the other prominent horsemen apparently said—you two gentlemen pick a name for the race. They decided to flip a coin to see for whom the race would be named. Fortunately Lord Derby won, and the rest is history. Can you imagine, what if Lutie had come back to America with the idea to name what has become "the most famous two minutes in sports"—The Kentucky Bunbury. It might never have become famous. The English Oaks and thus the Kentucky Oaks were easier to name—Lord Derby's estate was called "The Oaks". Sir Charles Bunbury, however, got his revenge when his colt Diomed won the first English Derby on May 4, 1780. Not only that, Diomed—after a mediocre stallion career in England—went to America at age twenty-one and became a foundation sire for the Kentucky Derby. His descendent Lexington was in the pedigree of fifty-two of the first sixty-one Derby winners (Note 2)

Colonel Clark no doubt learned much about the English system of purse money, racing rules, and wagering. It appears that Lutie did not like the bookie system of wagering. He undoubtedly learned more about the origin of the thoroughbred—stemming from breeding the stamina of slow English mares to the speedy Arabian stallions. At first the cross breeding was called thoroughly-bred. Eventually the English Jockey Club members decided to designate three stallions descended from Arabian lines to be the only sires to be used to determine a thoroughbred. They were: Herod, foaled in 1758, Matchem, foaled in 1748, and Eclipse, foaled in 1764 (during a total eclipse of the moon). (Note 3)

After months in England, Colonel Clark and his bride went to Paris, France. Although Lutie's wife was no doubt taken by the romantic aspects of Paris, he became fascinated by a new betting device called a "pari mutuel" machine. In French, "pari" means to wager and bet, and mutual means "between ourselves". (Note 4)

Ironically the machine had been invented by a Frenchman named Pierre Oller, who owned a perfume store in Paris. He also took some bets on horse races for his friends and customers, which he would sometimes send to bookies at the racetracks. When Oller started to lose heavily on bets that he kept, he realized that the track bookies were making bets with him, and manipulating the races to their advantage. (Note 5)

Oller invented his crude "pari mutual" machine in 1865 and operated it at his perfume store. The machine calculates all bets into a common pool, and the winning players split the proceeds—after five per cent is deducted for handling the money. This system is basically still used world-wide at racetracks—although the machines are now high-tech, and often customer operated. The track's handling per cent often runs 20 to 25 percent. The amount deducted usually is divided into thirds. One third each goes to the track for profit, the state for taxes, and to the races for purses.

In any case when Colonel Clark arrived at Longchamps Race Course in 1873, the machines were in use, and bookmakers had been ruled out. Ollers invention had become so popular that he even ran one at his perfume shop. Lutie, with his mathematical brain, immediately saw the potential to use "pari mutual" machines at his new idea of a race track in Louisville, Kentucky. Perhaps he would have liked to discuss the idea with his father Lewis, who was now commander of cadets, and professor of mathematics at the Kentucky Military Institute at Frankfort, Kentucky. Lutie could not pick up his cell phone, call dad and say—what do you think of this idea I have?

In any case, Colonel Clark headed back to America in the winter of 1873. Besides his wife, Lutie had four "pari mutual" machines that he had purchased. He was now fully armed and educated about racing in Europe, and anxious to start his dream race in Louisville, Kentucky. (Note 6)

Note 1, Frank G. Menke, *Churchill Downs and the Kentucky Derby,* (New York, NY, Churchill Downs-Latonia, Inc., 1942), Page 13.

Note 2, Peter Chew, *The Kentucky Derby-The First 100 Years,* (Boston, Mass, Houghton Mifflin, Co., 1974), Pages 5-7.

Note 3, Frank G. Menke, *Churchill Downs and the Kentucky Derby,* (New York, NY, Churchill Downs-Latonia, Inc., 1942), Page 6.

Note 4, Ibid, Page 14.

Note 5, Ibid, Pages 13-14.

Note 6, Ibid, Page 15.

CHAPTER 94

Colonel M. Lewis Clark Returns To His Old Kentucky Home

Lutie, with his precious cargo of four "pari mutual" machines—and his wife, arrived back in America from France during the winter of 1874. His head was full of ideas about how to jump-start thoroughbred racing in Kentucky. Arriving on the east coast of America by boat, the colonel was anxious to get home to Louisville as soon as possible. He was fortunate to have the opportunity to take advantage of another kind of horse—the iron horse. Perhaps he took a Baltimore and Ohio train (established in 1830) from New York or Baltimore to Cincinnati, Ohio, and then a Louisville and Nashville train (established in 1850) to Louisville. He could do in two days what his great grandparents had taken three months to do by horse and wagon from Virginia to Pittsburg, and then a flatboat down the Ohio River. Perhaps the trains gave Lutie another idea. Horses could now be transported from the east, or the west by rail—to run in his proposed big race in Louisville, Kentucky. (Note 1)

In any case Colonel Clark arrived back in Louisville in late winter of 1874. He immediately started to recruit investors for his idea of a race track, and some big purse money races—patterned after English racing. To this end, on June 22, 1874, Lutie held a meeting at the Galt House with a small group of Louisville businessmen (the Galt House being near its present location—with the original Galt House burning down in 1865 [now Bearnos By The Bridge-next to the great new arena—the Yum! Center]). (Note 2)

Colonel M. Lewis Clark was a promoter, and now a large man—hard to turn down as an investor. The colonel was perhaps lucky to be in the right place at the right time. The "River City" of Louisville was now thriving in the 1870's. The Louisville and Portland Canal had been Completed in 1830—making it possible for large steamboats to go up and down the Ohio River thru four locks for the twenty-four foot ascent or descent. (Note 3)

As the June meeting continued, Lutie convinced 320 men to put up $100 each to incorporate the Louisville Jockey Club and Driving Park Association. Colonel M. Lewis Clark was to be president and presiding judge. Lutie probably convinced some investors by proposing some big races at the new track—namely The Kentucky Derby, and The Kentucky Oaks—each at a mile and one half—similar to the English races. (Note 4)

Lutie also proposed a race at two miles for older horses—hopefully to be run at a fall meet—another of his ideas. He named this race the Clark Stakes—after himself. Why not, since the idea for the race came from the English St. Leger Stakes—named for another colonel—St. Leger. This race is now called the Clark Handicap, and is run every November at Churchill Downs. (Note 5)

With a bankroll of $32,000, and his uncles John and Henry Churchill as investors, Lutie convinced the men to lease the new corporation eighty acres of their holdings for the site of the track—in a rural area four and a half miles south of the city. As compensation for the use of the land, the brothers would receive $500 per year. (Note 6)

With the site acquired, and money in the corporation, Colonel Clark started to build his dream track. He supervised every detail of the grading of the one mile oval. Then came the bad news—by the time the track was finished to the Colonel's approval, the $32,000 was gone. Fortunately a local merchant came to Lutie's aid, and loaned the corporation enough money to build a grandstand, stables for four hundred horses, and a small clubhouse for investors/Jockey Club Members. All of the original structures were on the east side of the track—now familiarly known as the "backside". Colonel Clark planned to live in the clubhouse during race meets—in order to entertain Jockey Club members and their wives. (Note 7)

Note 1, KET—Kentucky's Story—*Riverboats and Railroads*—Program 8.

Note 2, Peter Chew, *The Kentucky Derby-The First 100 Years,* (Boston, Mass, Houghton Mifflin Co., 1974), Page 16.

Note 3, Samuel W. Thomas and Eugene H. Conner, T*he Journals of Increase Allen Lapham for 1827-1830,* (Louisville, KY, G. R. Clark Press, Inc., 1973), Page 111.

Note 4, Frank G. Menke, *Churchill Downs and The Kentucky Derby,* (New York, NY, Churchill Downs-Latonia, Inc., 1942), Page 15.

Note 5, Ibid, Page 15.

Note 6, Peter Chew, *The Kentucky Derby-The first 100 Years,* (Boston, Mass, Houghton Mifflin Co., 1974), Page 16.

Note 7, Ibid, Page 16.

CHAPTER 95

Colonel M. Lewis Clark Sets up Kentucky Racing and Betting Rules

In 1874 while the new track was being built under his supervision, Colonel Clark was also busy writing conditions for horses to enter his big races. The Kentucky Derby would be a race for three year colts, geldings, and fillies at a mile and one half (changed to its present distance of a mile and one quarter in 1896). The Kentucky Oaks would also be a mile and one half—but for three year old fillies only (changed to a mile and one quarter in 1892, to a mile and one sixteenth in 1896, and to its present distance of a mile and on eighth in 1920). (Note 1)

The Colonel now had a larger problem—which betting system to use to make the track a success. He wanted to use his "pari mutual" machines, and the currently popular system of auction pools. There were no bookies in Louisville in 1875. Furthermore, which system or systems would the State of Kentucky allow him to use?? In checking the laws of betting in Kentucky, Colonel Clark found out that any bank, keno, faro, or machine betting was illegal. (Note 2)

Auction pools were not mentioned, and were very popular in the Blue Grass region. An auction pool in racing is a scenario wherein each horse is auctioned off to the highest bidder—one at a time. If no bid is made on a horse, it becomes a member of the field. The total amount of all the bids is paid to the person who bought the winning horse—minus a fee of five per cent for handling the money.

Hoping to use his "pari mutual" machines at his race track, Lutie went to the Kentucky Legislature—which was fortunately in session in

Frankfort, the state capitol. Colonel Clark soon got an amendment to the anti-gambling law. The amendment allowed combination (auction) pools, or French ("pari mutual") pools at a race track during their racing season. Thus, race track wagering was legalized in Kentucky. This again shows the persuasive powers of Colonel Clark. In this case he was probably helped by some of the Kentucky Legislators also being investors in the new race track. Also, was his father Meriwether Lewis Clark, Sr. (Lewis) present during the proceedings? After all, Lewis was now a prominent citizen of Frankfort, Kentucky, and had possibly designed the building in which the meetings were held. (Note 3)

Now that "pari mutual" betting would be legal at his new track, Lutie was anxious to use his new machines there. He even set up a machine in the lobby of the Galt House Hotel so people could play with it, and see how it operated. Unfortunately, Colonel Clark was not able to use his new machines at his new track until 1878. This was possibly due to not being able to train enough people to operate the machines. It took two people—one to operate the machine, and one to sell the $5.00 win tickets. There is some evidence that the machines were at the track for the first Derby, but the patrons avoided them—preferring the tried and true auction pools. The number of auction pools was limited only by the demand of patrons to buy them. (Note 4)

With the "pari mutual" system of betting becoming more popular, the auction system died out by 1911. It is still alive and well, however, in two other sports. In most country club golf tournaments, the teams or individuals are auctioned off just as the races had been. Another popular auction is held for the sixty-four teams of the N. C. A. A. basketball tournament. These sport auctions are called "Calcuttas".

Besides the betting situation, Colonel Clark was involved in all aspects pertaining to the upcoming three day race meet. He had a large silver bowl made for the winner of the first Derby. Lutie also had silver pins made for members of the Jockey Club (the investors), to give them access to the track and the clubhouse. He also organized a ladies' committee to sew brightly colored silk purses. These purses would be hung on a wire at the finish line, and would contain the purse money. The winning jockeys would grab their purses from the wire on their way back to weigh out. (Note 5)

With all of the details seemingly worked out, Colonel M. Lewis Clark was no doubt anxious for opening day to come at his new track.

Would the people of Louisville come? At least he has fifteen starters for his first Kentucky Derby—from forty-two nominations at $50.00 each. This amounted to $2,100.00, and his Louisville Jockey Club would add $1,000, making a total purse of $3,100.00—a lot of money in 1875! The winner was to get $2,900.00, with second place receiving $200.00. (Note 6)

Note 1, Frank G. Menke, *Churchill Downs and the Kentucky Derby,* (New York, NY, Churchill Downs-Latonia, Inc., 1942), Page 15.

Note 2, Ibid, Page 14.

Note 3, Ibid, Page 15.

Note 4, Peter Chew, *The Kentucky Derby-The first 100 Years,* (Boston, Mass, Houghton Mifflin Co., 1974), Pages 16-17.

Note 5, Ibid, Page 17.

Note 6, Frank G. Menke, *Churchill Downs & the Kentucky Derby,* Ibid Pg 92

Chapter 96

The First Kentucky Derby—The Colonel's Dream Come True

On May 17, 1875, the first race meet was held at The Louisville Jockey Club track in Louisville, Kentucky. Besides the investors and their wives, the horsemen and their entourages, the people of Louisville came out in droves. They came by mule drawn trolley cars down Fourth Street, fringed-topped buggies, and every other means of transportation available.

The crowd eventually swelled to over ten thousand—far beyond the expectations of Colonel Clark. In the clubhouse, the ladies were dressed in the finery of the day, trailing long gowns, twirling parasols, and sipping lemonade. The Bluegrass horsemen were busy talking horses, and sipping mint juleps. (Note 1)

Finally it was time for the first race at 2:30 P. M. on Monday May 17, 1875—yes a Monday, not a Saturday. The *Courier Journal* newspaper had recommended that employers give their people a half-day holiday. The first race was a so called "sprint" of one and one quarter miles—with a purse of $300.00. In the early days of racing in Europe and America, most races were run in heats of three or four miles—and sometimes three out of five heats. (Note 2)

Finally Colonel Clark's dream was beginning to come true, as the fifteen well-bred three year old thoroughbreds stepped onto the track for the first Kentucky Derby. Lexington horseman and breeder H. P. McGrath's duo of Chesapeake and Aristides were the favorites—used as an entry in the auction pools. Chesapeake was considered the real favorite, since he had won the Lexington Stakes. Aristides had run poorly in the Phoenix Hotel Stakes in Lexington—and had cut his leg on the muddy track. Ironically, Aristides had been entered by McGrath as a "rabbit" for Chesapeake. A "rabbit" is a horse with speed but questionable stamina—entered to force an honest pace for a come from behind horse—which Chesapeake was.

The starter of races in 1875 did two things to start races after they had the field lined up behind the starting pole—he slammed down his red flag, and told an assistant to beat his drum. The drum was to help jockeys who might not be able to see the flag drop. As the flag dropped for the first Kentucky Derby, three of the fifteen horses wheeled—causing Chesapeake to rear and almost throw his rider. He was basically left at the post, with Aristides the "rabbit" soon in the lead. As they came to the stretch, H. P. McGrath waved to the jockey to go on if you can—your stable-mate is a no-show. After fighting off a late charge by Volcano and Verdigris, Aristides won by a length—in the fastest time ever run by a three-year-old in America at a mile and one half—2:37 ¾. (Note 3)

The third race of that opening day of racing was back to a series of five heats of one mile each. There were five entrants—with the winner of each heat to get $100.00. Next came the Kentucky Oaks—also run at a mile and one half. It was won by Vinagarette in a time exactly two seconds slower (about ten lengths) than the first Derby. The day was then capped off by the Clark Stakes at two miles—also for three-year-olds at the time. Ten Broeck, who later excelled at races of two, three, or four miles, finished fifth in the Derby—but should have opted for the Clark Stakes. (Note 4)

With the first day's racing successfully completed at the Louisville Jockey Club and Driving Association track, the partying in the new clubhouse went on late into the night—with champagne and mint juleps flowing freely. Colonel Clark, with his family, friends, and business associates, was no doubt enjoying the fruits of his labor. Was dad Lewis at age sixty-six with Lutie to enjoy his great accomplishment?

In any case, it was an amazing thing that Colonel Clark had done—starting the corporation on June 22, 1874, and then running the first day of racing on May 17, 1875—less than eleven months later. Lutie had also started many traditions that have continued without interruption, and are flourishing one hundred and thirty-seven years later. Yes the Belmont Stakes started in 1867, and the Preakness started in 1870, are older that the Kentucky Derby, but both were interrupted during World War II.

Note 1, Peter Chew, *The Kentucky Derby-The First Hundred Years,* (Boston, Mass, Houghton Mifflin Co., 1974), Page 23.

Note 2, Ibid, Page 23.

Note 3, Ibid, Pages 24-25.

Note 4, Frank G. Menke, *Churchill Downs and the Kentucky Derby,* (New York, NY, Churchill Downs-Latonia, Inc., 1942), Page 18.

Chapter 97

Meriwether Lewis Clark, Junior—The Original Kentucky Colonel

With the first Kentucky Derby and Oaks, and the first spring meet a success, Colonel Clark continued to promote the race track. He also wanted to start a fall meet at his Louisville Jockey Club course, but was never able to do so.

Colonel Clark continued to do a good job promoting the Kentucky Derby. By 1878 he also got his four pari-mutuel machines working to bet on the races. New York had beaten Kentucky by a year in using the machines. They called them "Paris Mutuels"—since they had come from Paris. The "s" was eventually dropped for some reason, and a "dash" added—making it the only system now used at race tracks, pari-mutuel betting. (Note 1)

To promote the Derby, Colonel Clark would hold lavish parties for visiting horsemen and dignitaries at his clubhouse at the track, and at The Pendennis Club in downtown Louisville. He even started the tradition of having mint juleps at his parties. He would mix a mint julep in a loving cup, present it to his guest of honor, have he or she take a sip and pass it on. In 1878 Clark's main guest was Madame Helena Modjeska, a Polish actress, and her husband was a count. Madame Modjeska took a sip of the mixture of bruised mint leaves, powdered sugar, crushed ice, and Kentucky bourbon—sighed with pleasure and continued sipping. She then told Clark: "This one, I will keep. You, please will make another for the Count". Thus, the tradition of the individual mint julep was born. (Note 2)

The origin of the mint julep is somewhat clouded. A book published in London in 1803, stated that Virginians took a dram of spirituous liquor steeped with mint in the morning. Henry Clay was born in Virginia and came to Lexington, Ky. in 1797. Later, as a Kentucky Senator, Henry Clay introduced the drink to Washington, D. C. at the famous Willard Hotel. Here again, Colonel Clark was ahead of his time, and probably served them at the first Derby in 1875. Now, over 120,000 mint juleps are served each year at Churchill Downs on Oaks and Derby day. (Note 3)

As the first years of the Kentucky Derby continued under the leadership of Colonel Clark, most things went smoothly—until the bookmakers showed up in 1882, and wanted a piece of the action. They were finally allowed to pay a fee to run their pools and the auction pools. Although bookies were finally ruled illegal in 1908, and auction pools lost their popularity by 1911, Colonel Clark had to deal with all three systems of betting during his tenure as President and Placing Judge. (Note 4)

Colonel M. Lewis Clark did many great things to initiate and name what is now the greatest thoroughbred race in America. Although he saved the dying breeding industry in Kentucky, founded the pari-mutuel system in America, and set racing rules that still exist, he did not give the track he started its now famous name. In 1886 a writer for a paper called the "Spirit of the Times" called it Churchill Downs. The name immediately became popular, and most people can not remember that it was originally called the "Louisville Jockey Club Course". Colonel Clark and his two uncles, John and Henry Churchill no doubt supported the new name—after all, the track was built on Churchill land.

Note 1, Frank G. Menke, *Churchill Downs and the Kentucky Derby,* (New York, NY, Churchill Downs-Latonia, Inc., 1942), Page 14.

Note 2, Peter Chew, *The Kentucky Derby-The First 100 Years,* (Boston, Mass, Houghton Mifflin, Co., 1974) Page 17.

Note 3, History of the Mint Julep—Wikipedia, the free encyclopedia.

Note 4, Frank G. Menke, *Churchill Downs and the Kentucky Derby,* (New York, NY, Churchill Downs-Latonia, Inc., 1942), Page 21.

Note 5, Ibid, Page 15.

CHAPTER 98

Colonel M. Lewis Clark in Demand-As a Racing Judge

During all race meets at Churchill Downs, Colonel Clark was very busy. Besides entertaining Jockey Club Members, and keeping a sharp eye on the betting systems, he was also the presiding judge. This meant that he must stay at the finish line to determine the winning horse—plus the second and third place finishers.

To do this judging task, Colonel Clark set up a small stand at the finish pole, twelve feet from the inner rail. He would then add vertical rods on each side of the track, and attach a tightly drawn string to the rods. Lutie would sit in a large chair directly in line with the rods, and site along the rope to determine the first three finishers. He would then write the numbers on a pad, sign it, and have two associate judges initial it. After the horses returned to the stand and faced the judge, the results would be declared official. For the first ten Derbies, all horses except the first three were bracketed in the charts as "also ran". Starting with the eleventh Derby in 1885, the official order of finish was listed for all of the horses—with the use of cameras. (Note 1)

As Colonel Clark gained more experience judging races, he became an expert in spotting suspicious looking bets by bookies, jockeys, or trainers. With his authority as judge, he would call all bets off, switch some jockeys to different horses, and give the patrons twenty minutes to remake their bets. (Note 2)

As Colonel Clark's reputation for honesty, integrity, and impartiality grew, he was in demand to judge races at other tracks—and did so when Churchill Downs was not running. For example, at Garfield Park in Chicago, Lutie received $100 per day, a carriage to take him to and from the track, a personal servant in the judge's stand, and his living expenses—which were considerable. Colonel Clark was living the good life as a Kentucky racing pioneer. (Note 3)

Although the Kentucky Derby was becoming more popular in America and around the world, it was not returning dividends to the investors. Lutie was putting most of the track's profit into improvements and increased purses for stakes. Colonel Clark's popularity was beginning to wane by 1893. Part of the problem was not his fault, as American horsemen were beginning to think running a mile and one half in May was too far for a three-year-old colt. In the twenty-first century, many horsemen think a mile and one quarter in May is too far. From 1890 to 1895 there were many Derby nominations, but the fields numbered only an average of less than five. (Note 4)

Lutie had also lost his father in October of 1881, and that was no doubt a distraction from his job as President and Presiding Judge at Churchill downs. Meriwether Lewis Clark, Sr. was laid to rest in Bellefontaine Cemetery in St. Louis, Missouri—next to his famous father, William Clark—as had been pre-arranged.

Another problem arose that greatly affected Louisville and the Kentucky Derby—the great tornado of March 27, 1890. With no warning sirens at the time, the tornado carved a path of destruction down Main Street to the end of town. Nearly eight hundred buildings were destroyed, and over one hundred people were killed. The Union Depot, the municipal water-works, plus a number of churches, homes, and small businesses were also destroyed. (Note 5)

Although Churchill Downs was not affected physically, the task of mourning the dead, and rebuilding the city, certainly put the sport of horse racing in Louisville on the back burner. Nevertheless, on May 14, 1890, some fans and six horses showed up for the 16th consecutive Kentucky Derby—amazingly, less than two months after the devastating tornado. Colonel Clark's race had survived for another year. (Note 6)

Note 1, Peter Chew, *The Kentucky Derby-The first 100 Years,* (Boston, Mass, Houghton Mifflin Co., 1974), Page 18.

Note 2, Ibid, Page 17.

Note 3, Ibid, Page 17.

Note 4, Frank G. Menke, *Churchill Downs and the Kentucky Derby,* (New York, NY, Churchill Downs-Latonia, 1942), Page 56.

Note 5, Kevin McQueen, *The Great Louisville Tornado of 1890,* (History Press, 2011).

Note 6, Frank G. Menke, *Churchill Downs and the Kentucky Derby,*(New York, NY, Churchill Downs-Latonia, 1942), Page 100.

CHAPTER 99

Colonel M. Lewis Clark Passes the Reins—And Passes On

Although Colonel Clark was known to be an honest and impartial judge at the race tracks, he was also known to have a hot temper—and he carried a gun. At times Lutie would threaten a person with his gun who had welched on a bet, not paid a racing fee, or had insulted his reputation or integrity. (Note 1)

In 1893 Colonel Clark suffered a serious blow to his financial situation—due to the stock market crash. It is very ironic that Lutie never owned any horses—always a gamble, or bet on horses. Yet he apparently invested heavily in the stock market and lost—the same thing as betting, but the results take longer than a race. (Note 2)

As Colonel Clark's problems escalated, he turned to his friend Charles Franklin Price—the brilliant City Editor of the Louisville *Post*. Lutie convinced Price to come to work at Churchill Downs as Racing Secretary. With the Derby fields shrinking, Churchill Downs was in danger of closing down. Thus, when an offer to buy the track came in the winter of 1893-1894, Colonel Clark and his associates decided to sell—for an undisclosed amount. Lutie, with his financial situation in disarray, had no choice but to sell. (Note 3)

Colonel Clark would remain at Churchill Downs as Presiding Judge until his death in 1899. Lutie's friend Charles F. Price would remain as Racing Secretary—one who writes the conditions for races to be run at a particular racetrack.

The new group of owners of Churchill Downs was incorporated as the New Louisville Jockey Club on August 11, 1894. They soon managed to raise $100,000 for changes and improvements to the track. Before the 1895 race meet, the new group had the old stands torn down, and a new grandstand built on the west side of the track. The old stands had been a constant irritation for fans—with the afternoon sun glaring in their eyes. The new stands were 285 feet long and mostly brick. They were highlighted by two steeples, rising above the new roof. The new stands could seat 1,500 people, and another 2,000 could stand on the wide steps leading to the seats—a no-no in today's world of fire prevention. The stands and the twin spires still exist in the twenty-first century, but are sadly dwarfed by the new high-rise six level structures on both sides of the old stands. (Note 4)

Along with the physical improvements at Churchill Downs, Racing Secretary Charles F. Price, seeing the decline of Derby runners, changed the distance to one mile and one quarter. This made an immediate improvement in entries for the Derby—namely 171 entries in 1896 versus 57 in 1895, and 55 in 1894. (Note 5)

As the American economy continued to decline late in the nineteenth century, Colonel Clark was also becoming more depressed with his situation. His Churchill family had deserted him due to his aggressive nature with guns, he had buried two wives, his health was failing, and he was now only a placing judge at the track he had started. On a trip to Memphis, Tennessee to discuss a new track there, Lutie apparently decided there was no use going on. He used his pistol on himself on April 22, 1899—there would be a new placing judge at the 25th Kentucky Derby on May 4, 1899. (Note 6)

Ironically, there were many things that Meriwether Lewis Clark, Junior and his namesake had in common—besides their famous names. They were both of undaunted courage, they both had great integrity, and they both accomplished great things. Unfortunately, they both also had hot tempers, which would cause them trouble at times. After becoming famous, both men would get in financial trouble and become depressed. Both men also carried guns, and unfortunately would use them upon themselves—ninety years apart—alone at an inn/hotel in different parts of Tennessee. The great accomplishments of both men have lived on in American history.

The demise of Colonel M. Lewis Clark only eleven days before the Derby, no doubt had a negative effect on the race. With the economy declining in 1899, and with no Colonel Clark present to judge the races, host parties, and serve mint juleps, only five horses showed up for the Derby—out of 151 nominations. (Note 7)

By 1902 things became so bad that Churchill Downs almost closed forever. At this point Charles Price, the Racing Secretary decided to ask his good friend for help to keep the track from closing. His name was Matt Winn, a successful Louisville businessman. (Note 8)

Note 1, Meriwether Lewis Clark, Jr.-Wikipedia, the free encyclopedia, Pg 1.

Note 2, Ibid, Page 1.

Note 3, Frank G. Menke, *Churchill Downs and the Kentucky Derby,* (New York, NY, Churchill Downs, Inc., 1942), Page 25-26.

Note 4, Ibid, Page 24.

Note 5, Ibid, Page 24.

Note 6, Meriwether Lewis Clark, Jr.—Wikipedia, the free encyclopedia

Note 7, Frank G. Menke, *Churchill Downs and the Kentucky Derby,* (New York, NY, Churchill Downs-Latonia, Inc., 1942), Page 103.

Note 8, Ibid, Page 25.

Chapter 100

Colonel Matt Winn Builds Upon Colonel Clark's Start

Matt Winn was born in Louisville on June 30, 1861, and attended St. Xavier's School until he was fourteen. At that age he went to the first Kentucky Derby in 1875. He watched the race from his father's grocery wagon on the infield—and never missed a Derby for the rest of his life. After going to a business school and graduating in 1876, Matt Winn pursued a number of careers—from a glass company, to a grocery firm, and then to a tailoring company—at which he became very successful. (Note 1)

When his lifelong friend Charles Price approached Matt Winn in 1902 about organizing a group to buy the struggling track, Colonel Winn was skeptical about the idea. With Price's urging, Matt Winn decided to discuss the idea with some of his Louisville business associates. They liked the scenario, and bought the track late in 1902 for a mere $40,000.00. They continued to lease the land from the Churchill family until 1906—when they bought the property. (Note 2)

One of the first things Colonel Winn did in 1903 was to build a clubhouse on the east side, next to the grandstand—just past the finish line. Just as Colonel Clark had done, the clubhouse would be used to entertain Jockey Club members, friends and dignitaries. Clark's original clubhouse on the west side (now the barn area) had been torn down in 1894. With Colonel Winn as Vice President and General Manager, Churchill Downs started to recover, and show a profit for its investors.

Matt Winn also soon tackled the problem of racing dates—in order to avoid conflicts with nearby tracks. (Note 3)

In 1908 another problem arose—almost closing Churchill Downs. Political enemies of Charles Grainger, a former mayor of Louisville, came into power in Louisville and Jefferson County. At this time, Grainger was President and an investor in Churchill Downs. The first thing the new regime did was to outlaw bookies in Louisville. Since bookies had taken over all of the betting since 1899, this meant disaster for the track! (Note 4)

Here again, Colonel Clark's work with the Kentucky Legislature saved the day for Churchill Downs. Colonel Winn found the old amendment that Lutie had gotten added to the state gambling laws. The amendment stated that combination (auction) pools and French (pari mutual) pools were legal at race tracks in Kentucky during their live race meets. (Note 5)

Colonel Winn and Secretary Price could train men to sell auction pools, but what about the pari mutual machines—they had not been used since 1886—when the bookies took over the betting. The four original pari-mutuel machines brought from Paris by Colonel Clark were finally located—but they were not in working order. Two more machines were found in New York, but had not been used since the 1870's. Next Colonel Winn had to hire a number of mechanics to get the machines operating again. (Note 6)

The machines required tickets, so the Colonel had some printed, perfected them, and had his signature added to avoid counterfeiting. Charles Price even had some four-page booklets printed to explain how pari-mutuels are calculated.

When Derby day came on May 5, 1908, the six machines performed well—two selling win tickets, two for place tickets, and two for show tickets. (All tickets were $5.00 at that time, but would later be reduced to $2.00). With a few minor problems, the machines worked very well—selling $33,980 worth of win tickets, $13,945 worth of place tickets, and $19,645 worth of show tickets. The auction pools added another $12,669 for a grand total of $80,239. Colonel Clark's machines had saved the day! The fans that bet on the Derby winner Stone Street were very happy, since he paid $123.60 for a $5.00 win ticket—far more than a bookie would have offered. As the spring meet continued for another ten days, a total of $598,570 was bet using the pari-mutuel machines. Colonel Clark's idea was here to stay in America. (Note 7)

The pari-mutuel system became so popular at Churchill Downs, that the auction pools faded away by 1911. The political enemies of the track had actually done racing a big favor by outlawing bookies at the track. Officials from other tracks soon started to come to study Churchill Downs new successful system of betting.

Charles Price (hired by Colonel Clark) would stay at Churchill Downs to serve honorably as Racing Secretary, Associate Judge, and from 1904 until his death in1941 as a Steward. (A Steward is one of a group of people who decide when to call for an inquiry in a race—and rule for any disqualification). (Note 8)

Colonel Matt Winn (hired by Charles Price) would remain at Churchill Downs in various capacities until he passed away in 1949—having been President from 1938 to 1949. He was a great promoter and was known as "Mr. Derby". He was basically responsible for making the Derby more popular for horsemen from the east and the west. Other good men such as Bill Corum, Wathen Knebelkamp, and Tom Meeker have added to the tradition that Colonel M. Lewis Clark started—"The greatest two minutes in sports".

Note 1, Frank g. Menke, *Churchill Downs and the Kentucky Derby,* (New York, NY, Churchill Downs-Latonia, Inc., 1942), Page 24.

Note 2, Ibid, Page 25-26.

Note 3, Ibid, Page 26-28.

Note 4, Ibid, Page 30.

Note 5, Ibid, Page 31.

Note 6, Ibid, Page 31.

Note 7, Ibid, Page 37-38.

Note 8, Ibid, Page 23.

EPILOGUE

The Clarks of Kentucky Leave Their Mark on America

The last of the famous part of the Clark family was gone just before the start of the twentieth century, but the accomplishments of the first four generations of Clarks of Kentucky still live on in the twenty-first century.

The Clark legacy started when John Clark married Ann Rogers, and they produced ten children in Virginia, and started to raise them there. All of the living children would eventually move to Kentucky, and raise more children in Louisville.

Jonathan Clark, the first child was born in 1750. He would eventually become a general and help George Washington win the Revolution in the east. Brothers John and Edmund became Captains and also fought in the Revolution.

George Rogers Clark, the second child was born in 1752. He too would become a general and become famous by winning the Revolution in the west. This would basically add the Old Northwest Territory to America—consisting of many states. George would become the founder of Louisville, and help Kentucky obtain statehood.

William Clark, John and Ann Rogers Clark's ninth child, was born in 1770—making him almost eighteen years younger than his famous brother George. William would become famous by joining Meriwether Lewis to explore the Louisiana Purchase to the west coast, and later help to develop it. This would eventually add more states to America—west of the Mississippi River. He would then have a long and successful career serving five presidents as an Indian diplomat, while operating out of St. Louis. He would also help Missouri become a state.

William Clark's son, Meriwether Lewis Clark (Lewis) would go to West Point, become a successful architect in St. Louis, and later in Frankfort, Ky. He would fight in the Mexican War, the conclusion of which would add the rest of the states to the west coast of America from Spain, that were not included in the Louisiana Purchase.

Thus, you might say that the Clarks of Kentucky had their hand in helping to create the states and territories that would eventually total forty-six—with Washington and Oregon added later in a treaty with Canada.

Lewis' son, Meriwether Lewis Clark, Jr. (Lutie) would grow up in Louisville after the death of his mother. He would get involved with thoroughbred racing due to living with his uncles—John and Henry Churchill. He would eventually resurrect the Kentucky racing and breeding industries by starting Churchill Downs and the Kentucky Derby. He also became the father of pari-mutuel wagering in America—starting with his crude machines from Paris, France. Lutie also set up many rules of racing that are still in use today. Lutie was basically the first well known Kentucky Colonel, and also made the mint julep popular in Kentucky and elsewhere.

The female side of the original Clarks of Kentucky also added much to the Clark legacy. After Lucy Clark, born in 1765, married William Croghan (pronounced "Crawn"), they built Locust Grove and added nine children to the Clark bloodlines. Ann Clark, born in 1755, married Owen Gwathmey in Virginia, eventually moved to Kentucky, and added eleven children to the Clark line. Elizabeth Clark, born in 1773, added a total of seven more children to the Clark lineage.

Jonathan Clark would eventually move to Kentucky with his wife Sarah and their seven children. He would live out his life at his plantation in the Highlands of Louisville called Trough Spring. Although it has been changed greatly, Trough Spring still exists, but is a private residence. Letters from William Clark to brother Jonathan during the Lewis and Clark expedition give us much of what we know about the trip. Locust Grove and Trough Spring are the only two structures that still exist—that were built by the original Clarks of Kentucky.

It does seem sad that the first Clark house, Mulberry Hill, and the first structure in Louisville—the unnamed fort at 12th and

Rowan Streets have no original or rebuild structures on either site—to commemorate these two historic sites in Louisville.

At least, the site of Mulberry Hill is a part of George Rogers Clark Park on Poplar Level Road—just across from St. Xavier High School. There is only a family cemetery and one lone cypress tree left from the remains of Mulberry Hill. In a simple wire fenced in area, there are two full length granite slabs—under which lie the remains of John Clark and Ann Rogers Clark—the patriarch and matriarch of the famous Clarks of Kentucky.

BIBLIOGRAPHY

Ambrose, Stephen E. *To America,* New York, NY: Simon & Schuster, 2002.

Ambrose, Stephen E. *Undaunted Courage,* New York, NY: Simon & Schuster, 1996.

Baird, Clay P. *A Journey to the Falls,* Louisville, KY: Pinaire Lithographing Corporation, 1976.

Buckley, Jay H. *William Clark-Indian Diplomat,* Norman, OK: The University of Oklahoma Press, 2008.

Cerami, Charles A. *Jefferson's Great Gamble,* Naperville, IL: Sourcebooks, 2003.

Chew, Peter. *The Kentucky Derby-The First 100 Years,* Boston, Mass: Houghton Mifflin Company, 1974.

Clark, Thomas D. *A History of Kentucky,* New York, NY: Prentice-Hall, 1937.

Clark, Thomas D. *Simon Kenton: Kentucky Scout,* New York, NY: Farrar & Rinehart, 1943.

Coleman, J. Winston, Jr. *KENTUCKY-A Pictorial History,* Lexington, KY: The University Press of Kentucky, 1971.

De Voto, Bernard. *The Journals of Lewis and Clark,* New York, NY: Houghton Mifflin Company, 1953.

Griffin, Susan. *On the Threshold of Discovery,* Louisville, KY: Publisher's Press, Incorporated, 2003.

Harrison, Lowell H. *George Rogers Clark and the War in the West,* Lexington,KY: The University Press of Kentucky, 1976.

Haynie, Miriam. *The Stronghold,* Richmond, VA: The Dietz Press, Incorporated, 1959.

Holmberg, James J. *The Clark Family and the Kentucky Derby,* Louisville, KY: The Filson Historical Society Newsmagazine, Vol. 4, No 1.

Jennings, Kathleen. *Louisville's First Families: a Series of Genealogical Sketches,* Louisville, KY: The Standard Printing Company, 1920.

Ketchum, Richard M. *The Civil War,* New York, NY: American Heritage Publishing Company, Incorporated,1960.

McQueen, Keven. *The Great Louisville Tornado of 1890,* 2010.

Menke, Frank G. *Churchill Downs and The Kentucky Derby,* New York, NY: Churchill Downs-Latonia, Incorporated, 1942.

Ramage, James A. *Gray Ghost,* Lexington, KY: The University Press of Kentucky, 1999.

Riebel, R. C. *Louisville Panorama,* Louisville, KY: Liberty National Bank and Trust Company of Louisville, 1954.

Thomas, Samuel W. *The Journals of Increase Allen Lapham for 1827-1830,* Louisville, KY: G. R. Clark Press, Incorporated, 1973.

Tubbs, Stephanie Ambrose, with Jenkinson, Clay Straus. *The Lewis and Clark Companion,* New York, NY: Henry Holt and Company, LLC, 2003

Wikipedia, the free encyclopedia:
Boone, Daniel.

Bunbury, Sir Charles
Chief Big White
Chief Blackhawk
Clark, George Rogers.
Clark, Meriwether Lewis, Sr.
Clark, Meriwether Lewis, Jr.
Clark, William.
Derby, 12th Lord of
Harrod, James.
Kenton, Simon.
Mexican-American War.
Mint Julep.
Redstone Old Fort.
Taylor, Zachary.
Washington, Charles.

Yater, George H., *Two Hundred Years at the Falls of the Ohio,* Louisville, KY: The Heritage Corporation, 1979.